Managerial Skills

[Focusses on: Interpersonal Skills, Strategic and Lateral Thinking, Facing Changes and Challenges, Staying Motivated, Effective Decision Making, Conflict Resolution, Leadership Communication, Human Network, CSR, Professional Ethics, Workplace/Office Politics, Planning for a Second Career]

Dr. K. ALEX
Ph.D.
Associate Professor
St. Joseph's College,
Tiruchirapalli, Tamil Nadu

S. CHAND & COMPANY PVT. LTD.
(AN ISO 9001 : 2008 COMPANY)
RAM NAGAR, NEW DELHI - 110 055

S.CHAND
PUBLISHING
empowering minds

S. CHAND & COMPANY PVT. LTD.

(An ISO 9001 : 2008 Company)

Head Office: 7361, RAM NAGAR, NEW DELHI - 110 055
Phone: 23672080-81-82, 9899107446, 9911310888 Fax: 91-11-23677446
www.schandpublishing.com; e-mail: helpdesk@schandpublishing.com

Branches

Ahmedabad : Ph: 27541965, 27542369, ahmedabad@schandpublishing.com
Bengaluru : Ph: 22268048, 22354008, bangalore@schandpublishing.com
Bhopal : Ph: 4274723, 4209587, bhopal@schandpublishing.com
Chandigarh : Ph: 2725443, 2725446, chandigarh@schandpublishing.com
Chennai : Ph. 28410027, 28410058, chennai@schandpublishing.com
Coimbatore : Ph: 2323620, 4217136, coimbatore@schandpublishing.com (Marketing Office)
Cuttack : Ph: 2332580; 2332581, cuttack@schandpublishing.com
Dehradun : Ph: 2711101, 2710861, dehradun@schandpublishing.com
Guwahati : Ph: 2738811, 2735640, guwahati@schandpublishing.com
Hyderabad : Ph: 27550194, 27550195, hyderabad@schandpublishing.com
Jaipur : Ph: 2219175, 2219176, jaipur@schandpublishing.com
Jalandhar : Ph: 2401630, 5000630, jalandhar@schandpublishing.com
Kochi : Ph: 2378740, 2378207-08, cochin@schandpublishing.com
Kolkata : Ph: 22367459, 22373914, kolkata@schandpublishing.com
Lucknow : Ph: 4026791, 4065646 lucknow@schandpublishing.com
Mumbai : Ph: 22690881, 22610885, mumbai@schandpublishing.com
Nagpur : Ph: 6451311, 2720523, 2777666, nagpur@schandpublishing.com
Patna : Ph: 2300489, 2302100, patna@schandpublishing.com
Pune : Ph: 64017298, pune@schandpublishing.com
Raipur : Ph: 2443142, raipur@schandpublishing.com (Marketing Office)
Ranchi : Ph: 2361178, ranchi@schandpublishing.com
Siliguri : Ph: 2520750, siliguri@schandpublishing.com (Marketing Office)
Visakhapatnam : Ph: 2782609 visakhapatnam@schandpublishing.com (Marketing Office)

First Edition 2013
Reprint 2016

ISBN : 978-81-219-9869-7 **Code :** 1001 463

This book is for Sale in India & other SAARC Countries only.

PRINTED IN INDIA

By Vikas Publishing House Pvt. Ltd., Plot 20/4, Site-IV, Industrial Area Sahibabad, Ghaziabad-201010 and Published by S.Chand & Company Pvt. Ltd., 7361, Ram Nagar, New Delhi -110 055.

This Book is Dedicated to

Rev. Fr. K. Amal SJ,

&

Rev. Sr. K. Leema FIHM

Preface

To be called a manager you need to have a set of skills ranging from planning,organising, and directing to controlling. Whether you manage a business enterprise, an NGO or educational institutions you need to get the work done and to get the work done you need to possess some skills. In fact to emerge as a successful manager, you have to have these skills which form the baseline for a successful career path. These skills, in the modern world, are called Managerial Skills.

In the case of Sachin Tendulkar, runs came naturally to him, where as in the case of Rahul Dravid, he had to work hard for every run (as told by Rahul Dravid in an interview). But, in the end, both turned out to be great players. Similarly, either you are born with some managerial skills or you acquire them by constant and conscious efforts.

If you are born with some managerial skills thank the Super Power, if not, start believing that managerial skills can very well be acquired. The very fact that there are numerous B Schools in the world is a proof that Managerial Skills can be acquired. Acquiring managerial skills has become so important because work place has become pressure bound due to cut throat competition, delicate work force, scarcity of raw material, global melt down, volatile economy and so on.

To overcome the hurdles mentioned above you need to be familiar with the following basic managerial skills - conceptual skills, human skills and technical skills. These three can further be classified into intra personal relationship strategies, interpersonal relationship strategies, thinking strategies, execution strategies and behaviour strategies.

This book intends to throw light on the above mentioned topics besides, topics like lateral thinking, decision making, balancing work and life, corporate social responsibility, work ethics and planning for a second career.

This book is largely based on the author's hands-on experience as a corporate trainer for a period of almost two decades.The book is rich in content, having apt pictures, boxed items and figures to highlight the points discussed.

The readers by going through these topics, can learn the art of getting things done in a more relaxed and confident way. This book will help the readers to out shine their weaknesses and become awesome managers.

E-mail Id. alexkrr2002 @ yahoo.co.in

Dr. K. Alex

Acknowledgement

I would like to take this opportunity to thank few people who helped me make this dream a reality. At home, I want to acknowledge the support of my wife during the many hours I spent working on this book. I also like to acknowledge the sacrifices made by my children by foregoing their fun and frolic staying at home almost on all holidays for a year as I was not available to them.

I thank all my family members who had been a source of inspiration thus rendering me adequate inputs to get this book ready. I also would like to thank the Jesuits, particularly the Administrators in St.Joseph's College, Tiruchirapalli for being with me in my entire endeavour.

I also place on record my special thanks to my friends, well wishers, Principals, Correspondents, Secretaries and Founders of various colleges in India who invite me to address their staff and students. My special thanks are also due to Rotary Clubs, Lions Clubs, Leo Clubs, NGOs and various forums.

I am thankful to the Management Team and the Editorial Department of S. Chand & Company Pvt. Ltd. for all help and support in the publication of this book.

I have used some texts and exercises that either were given to me, during the training programmes attended at regular intervals, by trainers, or received from various group members like HR India, Leadership Groups, Hum aur Tum, Touch n Inspire, Nubia, of yahoo, for which the source is untraceable. I would like to acknowledge the original authors of those texts and exercises, but unfortunately, I am unable to locate the original sources. I would also like to acknowledge the various web sites for the pictorial illustrations that I have used in this text. Subject to objections raised from any of the sources, I would most willingly acknowledge the use of the material explicitly or withdraw the same as the case may be.

Dr. K. Alex

E-mail Id. alexkrr2002 @ yahoo.co.in

Contents

Managing Self

LEARNING OUTCOME

- Introduction
- Aristotle on Self
- Gender and Self
- Feminist Self
- Escaping the Self
- Importance of knowing oneself
- Process of knowing oneself
- SWOT Analysis
- Self Esteem
- Factors determining self esteem
- Factors determining one's self esteem at work place
- Characters associated with people having High self-esteem
- Characters associated with people having Low self-esteem
- Ways to improve one's self-esteem

Success is a fight between You and your Self

Introduction

Knowing others is knowledge and knowing self is wisdom, said Socrates. The biggest asset an individual has is the knowledge of himself/herself. Life is a journey of travelling within. Probably the longest journey possible by an individual is the journey within. Knowing oneself is the process of travelling within. Anyone who intends to conquer others will have to first conquer himself as it is the basis for all knowledge.

Before going into the topic know thyself/yourself , one should know the term the self. Self means defining of one's essential qualities that make one distinct from the other. Self is the agent responsible for the thoughts and actions of an individual. It is exhibited in the conduct and communication of that individual. The particular characteristics of an individual which determine his or her identity is known as self.

Self as proclaimed by Michael Walters

According to Michael Walters there are three kinds of self. They are

1. Perceived Self is how a person assesses himself and how he thinks others view him. (How am I understood by others)
2. Real Self is how the person really is. (What am I actually)
3. Ideal Self is how the person would like to be. (What do I want to be)

Self as proclaimed by Ulrich

According to Ulrich there are five different types of selves that you gradually become aware of as you grow. Each self presents different aspects of self. They differ in their origins and histories and in the manner in which they contribute to your experience. The five selves are

1. **The ecological self.** It is the self as perceived with respect to the physical environment. It refers to the environment you work in.
2. **The interpersonal self.** It refers to the emotional part of you, for i.e. the way you relate with others and the manner in which you communicate.
3. **The extended self.** It refers to your personal memories and the anticipations you make based on such memories.
4. **The private self.** It refers to that part of you that you have not shared with anyone. Pain and pleasure you alone experience.
5. **The conceptual self.** It refers to the assumptions, belief, faith that you hold on various aspects like the birth, the death, the God, the universe, the origin of human race and so on. There is a remarkable variety in what people believe about the above and not all of them are true.

Self as proclaimed by Kahlil Gibran

THE SEVEN SELVES (presented as given by him)

In the stillest hour of the night, as I lay half asleep, my seven selves sat together and thus conversed in whisper.

First Self: Here, in this madman, I have dwelt all these years, with naught to do but renew his pain by day and recreate his sorrow by night. I can bear my fate no longer, and now I rebel.

Second Self: Yours is a better lot than mine, brother, for it is given to me to be this madman's joyous self. I laugh his laughter and sing his happy hours, and with thrice winged feet I dance his brighter thoughts. It is I that would rebel against my weary existence.

Third Self: And what of me, the love-ridden self, the flaming brand of wild passion and fantastic desires? It is I the love-sick self who would rebel against this madman.

Fourth Self: I, amongst you all, am the most miserable, for naught was given me but odious hatred and destructive loathing. It is I, the tempest-like self, the one born in the black caves of Hell, who would protest against serving this madman.

Fifth Self: Nay, it is I, the thinking self, the fanciful self, the self of hunger and thirst, the one doomed to wander without rest in search of unknown things and things not yet created; it is I, not you, who would rebel.

Sixth Self: And I, the working self, the pitiful labourer, who, with patient hands, and longing eyes, fashion the days into images and give the formless elements new and eternal forms-it is I, the solitary one, who would rebel against this restless madman.

Seventh Self: How strange that you all would rebel against this man, because each and every one of you has a preordained fate to fulfil. Ah! could I but be like one of you, a self with a determined lot! But I have none, I am the do-nothing self, the one who sits in the dumb, empty nowhere and nowhen, while you are busy re-creating life. Is it you or I, neighbours, who should rebel?

When the seventh self thus spoke, the other six selves looked with pity upon him but said nothing more; and as the night grew deeper one after the other went to sleep enfolded with a new and happy submission.

But the seventh self remained watching and gazing at nothingness, which is behind all things.

Kahlil Gibran on Self Knowledge (as was told by him)

And a man said, "Speak to us of Self-Knowledge."

And he answered, saying:

Your hearts know in silence the secrets of the days and the nights.

But your ears thirst for the sound of your heart's knowledge.

You would know in words that which you have always know in thought.

You would touch with your fingers the naked body of your dreams.

And it is well you should.

The hidden well-spring of your soul must needs rise and run murmuring to the sea;

And the treasure of your infinite depths would be revealed to your eyes.

But let there be no scales to weigh your unknown treasure;

And seek not the depths of your knowledge with staff or sounding line.

For self is a sea boundless and measureless.

Say not, "I have found the truth," but rather, "I have found a truth."

Say not, "I have found the path of the soul." Say rather, "I have met the soul walking upon my path."

For the soul walks upon all paths. The soul walks not upon a line, neither does it grow like a reed. The soul unfolds itself, like a lotus of countless petals.

Aristotle on Self

Aristotle advocated that there were four sections of the soul. The four sections are

(i) calculative part,

(ii) the scientific part,

(iii) the desiderative part and

(iv) the vegetative part.

> You need a force to conquer others and strength to conquer yourself

Gender and Self

Men and women have differences in their thinking and the things they like. Women are said to have a self concept that is interdependent which are relationship oriented. They rely upon friends, loved ones and family, where as men are said to have self concept that focuses on large scale groups like being a member in clubs, forums and teams. Following observations are made with regard to gender and self.

> If you do not conquer SELF you will be conquered by SELF

1. **Physical appearance.** It is believed that appearance plays a significant role in determining self esteem of a woman than a man.

2. **Academics.** It is found that women perform better academically and get better grades than male peers.

3. **Social acceptance.** Women like to be in smaller groups and maintain more intimate relationship as against men who like to be in a larger groups and maintain not so deeper relationship.

4. **Family.** Family relationship has a significant impact on women self as compared to men.

5. Affect. Women are reported to be feeling more angry, anxious, depressed and stressed than their male counterparts.

6. Personal self. Women are said to be having low self esteem as they are less assertive and autonomous when compared to men particularly in the Indian context.

7. Satisfaction. Women are said to be more satisfied in life than men.

8. Moral and ethical. Studies reveal that women exhibit more moral maturity than men.

> The most difficult phase of life is not when no one understands you. It is when you don't understand yourself.

Feminist Self

It is believed that feminist self is subordinated and belittled since women have been understood as inferior to men. Hence efforts have to be made to establish women's selfhood. The goal of feminism should be

(i) To demonstrate the importance of women

(ii) To bring out gender equity

(iii) To reveal that women have been suffering as subordinates to men

(iv) To establish equality in opportunities

Escaping the Self

> No one can give you better advice than yourself.
>
> – Cicero

Sometimes people involve in some activities to get away from the kind of life they lead and the sufferings they undergo. Generally these activities are harmless i.e. developing a hobby, playing, swimming, watching TV, cinema and so on. Sometimes these activities are harmful and hazardous and prove to be fatal i.e. smoking , drinking, narcotics, suicide and so on.

These are the people who have not accepted them as they are, people who are unhappy with themselves, people who said to have low self esteem and are said to be avoiding any self introspection. Avoiding introspection generally leads to destructive behaviour such as using drugs, alcohol, smoking and suicidal tendencies.

In short, people try to escape from the situations they live in but the fact is that one cannot escape from realities.

Importance of knowing oneself

> If you don't know what you are building, no tool will help.

There are some people in the world who do not know who they are and there are few others who do not want to know who they are. But it is very important to know who you are.

Knowing oneself takes years of soul searching and insight. It is a process of stripping away the masks that people put on and getting down to the core of one's essence.

Knowing oneself will help an individual to handle the challenges that life hands him/her. It also helps persons to make better decisions. Knowing oneself helps the individuals to reach their goals more effectively and leads to the path of success. The deeper the knowledge of self, the more comfortable one feels with himself and others.

The following points will throw more light on the importance of knowing oneself.

1. Helps to control emotions

Knowing yourself guards yourself against your responses triggered by your emotions. Everything you do is based on your emotions only and often emotions lead to miscalculations. Knowing yourself helps you to take control of your emotions and helps in decisions and choices when you are in an emotional state.

2. Helps to reach your goal

Knowing yourself is a very important task that you have to undertake, and the most challenging as well. When you know who you are, and clearly understand what you want, you have a better chance of discovering how to reach your goal, personal fulfillment and happiness.

3. Helps to reach better decisions

Knowing yourself is important because it will help you to make better decisions and be a better person. The more aware you are of your faults the less detached you will feel. You will also feel more at ease with yourself. You will also be able to improve those things that you want to and let go of the things that you can't.

4. Helps to improve relationship

Knowing your true and inner self will be of great help in working to reach your goals more effectively. It will guide you along the path to success and take you to such calmness that it will improve your attitude as well as your relationships with others in your life.

5. Helps to realize and improve your full potential

Knowing yourself will enable you to develop your full potential and be happy, contented and fulfilled. Knowing yourself ensures success in business, friendship, love, sports, or altogether.

6. Helps to experience happiness and joy

Knowing yourself enables you to discover and attain your goals and then when you reach your goals you turn out to be a happy person. This not only fills you with much happiness but also improves your mindset. And that is the happiness in the truest sense.

Process of knowing oneself

1. Maintain personal diary

Maintaining a diary helps you in learning what you are, your likes and dislikes, your passions, and what you want to be in life. Find five to ten minutes every day and choose a comfortable place to write. Write about how you feel, what bothers you, what excites you, and establish a connection between you and yourself.

2. Practice meditation

Meditation helps you to observe yourself in the present moment. Often meditation is misunderstood to be a tough practice and only the sadhus and sanyasis can perform it. It is not so. Meditation is not a state of emptying the mind but emptying yourself of anxiety, worry, excitement and so on. Find 10 minutes every day and sit comfortably. Focus on your breath and allow the thoughts that enter your mind. Acknowledge them but don't allow them to disturb you.

3. Exercise regularly

It is proved time and again that exercise helps a person physically and mentally. Exercise is a kind of meditation. It helps you in different ways. If you are a person facing hard times then exercise is the best way to slow you down.

4. Go for walk regularly

If exercising is not possible, opt for walking because walking is a moving mediation. It allows you to slow down, and notice what's going on around you. It can provide you with an opportunity to mull over something that may be on your mind, or simply to notice the beauty and bounty of what surrounds you.

5. Do some riding or driving

This may look a bit odd here. But driving proves to be a good process particularly when you find it hard to locate a quiet place. Do not forget to take your electronic gadgets to listen to your favourite music.

6. Do some outings

Practice a habit of going out for sight seeing particularly when down with something in life. A day spent in the park, a theatre, coffee house and so on help a lot. These are the outings that allow you to be with yourself. The purpose of these activities is sheer enjoyment.

7. Develop some hobbies

Identify the hobbies of your early days. Try to do things that you used to do those days. It will give you a chance to identify your passion within you. After all what was done in the early days has a lot of impact in a person's life. Hobbies help you to find some time to relax.

8. Develop new interests

As the days pass by in the school, colleges, or offices develop new interest. Allow yourself to think something new and different. Such thinking may take you sky high in the ladder of your personal and professional life. Investigate and research things you find interesting. Try connecting ideas that come across your mind and continuously explore.

SWOT Analysis

SWOT stands for Strengths, Weaknesses, Opportunities and Threats.

A SWOT analysis is a framework for analyzing your strengths and weaknesses, and the opportunities and threats you face. This helps you to focus on your strengths, minimize weaknesses, and take the greatest possible advantage of opportunities available.

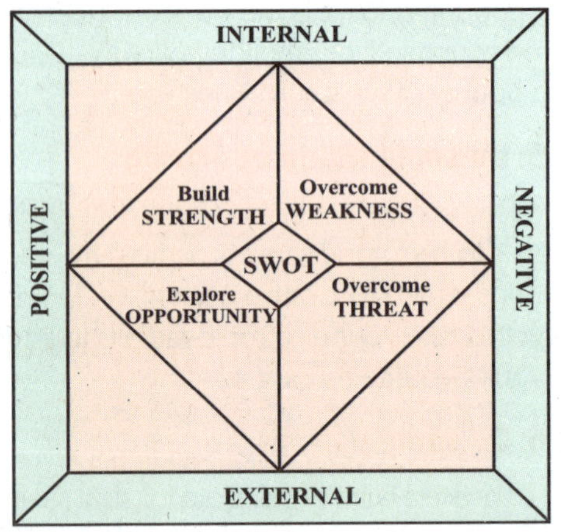

A SWOT analysis is particularly powerful that it can help you uncover opportunities that you can take advantage of. And by understanding your weaknesses, you can manage and eliminate threats that would otherwise put you in difficulties.

> ***No one can give you better advice than yourself.*** – Cicero

Benefits of SWOT analysis

One of the major benefits of a SWOT analysis is that it is scaleable. It can be as small as a couple of people talking about a situation to a multi-month project in a large multinational company. The other benefits are:

- **Simple.** It's simple to the participants. They can grasp the concepts and process easily. And, they almost always enjoy the process. It can be practiced at individual and corporate level.
- **Less expensive**. A SWOT analysis can be done internally provided the internal facilitator has the experience to manage it. The basic SWOT technique can be fashioned to meet individual as well as corporate needs.
- **Inclusive**. It allows the participation of the team. In addition, since it utilizes the whole team, the results are more likely to represent the real environments.

Using SWOT analysis

When using SWOT analysis, be realistic about the strengths and weaknesses of you. Distinguish between where you are today, and where you could be in the future. Also remember to be specific by avoiding grey areas and always analyze in relation to the actual situation. Finally, keep your SWOT analysis short and simple, and avoid complexity and over-analysis. Use it as a guide and not a prescription.

Swot analysis grid

A SWOT analysis is typically created in a grid format, with the Strengths and Opportunities listed on the left, and the Weaknesses and Threats on the right.

> ***Knowing others is intelligence; knowing yourself is wisdom.***
>
> ***Mastering others is strength; mastering yourself is power.*** – Tao Te Ching

Strengths	Weaknesses
1. 2. 3. 4. 5.	1. 2. 3. 4. 5.
Opportunities	**Threats**
1. 2. 3. 4. 5.	1. 2. 3. 4. 5.

Questions to complete the grid

Strengths:

What do you do well?

What unique resources can you draw on?

What do others see as your strengths?

Weaknesses:

What could you improve?

Where do you have fewer resources than others?

What are others likely to see as weaknesses?

Opportunities:

What good opportunities are open to you?

What trends could you take advantage of?

How can you turn your strengths into opportunities?

Threats:

What trends could harm you?

What is your competition doing?

Self Esteem

Self-esteem is a phrase used to reflect a person's overall appraisal of his worth that includes his beliefs and emotions. It includes terms like self belief, self-worth, self-regard, self-respect and self-integrity.

Self esteem means loving and feeling good about oneself unconditionally. Self esteem is that feeling at the centre of one's being of self-worth, self-confidence, and self-respect. High self esteem means that one feels good about himself.

> Those who can't laugh at themselves leave the job to others.

Self esteem is the opinion of oneself. High self esteem is a good opinion of oneself and low self esteem is a bad opinion of oneself. High self-esteem is a positive opinion and low self-esteem is a negative opinion on oneself.

Self-esteem can involve a variety of beliefs about the self, such as the appraisal of one's own appearance, beliefs, emotions and behaviours.

Factors determining self esteem

1. One's nature

From the birth, people are influence by their perceptions and predispositions about persons and things.

2. One's nurture

Nurture refers to the environmental influences that play a role in shaping one's personality. Significant factors are family, social and economic status, education, the role of religion, and people you encountered.

3. One's Locus of Evaluation

It is the reference point one uses to evaluate his worth. It is the source from which one seeks approval for his behaviours and existence. Locus of evaluation tends to be either external e.g. the society, internal e.g. the voice within or a mixture of both.

4. Self Talk

Self talk is comprised of one's thoughts, beliefs and attitudes. It is this internal chatter that defines one's self esteem. If the beliefs and attitudes are positive and healthy then one will have favourable self esteem. If the thoughts and views are self limiting then you will have negative self esteem.

> A man travels the world over in search of what he needs and returns home to find it.
>
> – George Moore

Factors determining one's self esteem at work place are

The ability to relate with others
The knowledge of one's strength and weakness
The respect given for the work done
The social status enjoyed
The way one sees himself
The worth of the job

Characters associated with people having High self-esteem

- Are good with other people.
- Are nice and friendly to people.
- Being able to solve any challenges
- Believe in their abilities to achieve what they want.
- Completely accepts themselves.
- Feel worthy of love and approval.
- Have a sense of humour
- Have an opinion and are not afraid of sharing it.
- Know their strengths and weaknesses.
- Know themselves very well.

- Know what is important to them in life.
- Know what they want in life.
- Know what they will and will not accept.
- Know where they come from
- Know where they're going.
- Know who they are
- Love life
- Willing to move out of their comfort zones

> It is not only the most difficult thing to know oneself, but the most inconvenient one, too.
>
> –H.W. Shaw

In short

1. Firm belief in certain values and principles
2. Trust in their ability to judge
3. Not worrying unnecessarily
4. Considering themselves equal to others in capacities
5. Accepts the shortcomings
6. Involved in various activities
7. Sensitive to needs and feelings of others

Characters associated with people having Low self-esteem

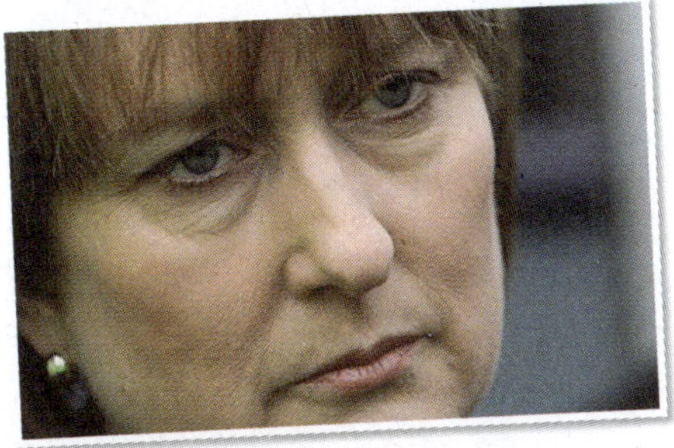

1. Accentuating the negative
2. An Inability to see oneself squarely
3. Anxiety and emotional turmoil
4. Eating disorders
5. Concern over what others think of you
6. Expecting little out of life for yourself
7. Inability to accept compliments
8. Lack of social skills
9. Lack of self confidence
10. Less social conformity
11. Reluctance to put yourself anywhere
12. Reluctance to take on challenges
13. Reluctance to trust your own opinion
14. Self neglect
15. Social withdrawal
16. Treating yourself badly but NOT other people
17. Worrying whether you have treated others badly

> There are three things extremely hard: steel, a diamond, and to know one's self.
>
> Benjamin Franklin

In short

1. A state of dissatisfaction
2. Hard to accept criticism
3. Fear of making mistakes
4. Tendency to please everyone
5. Looking for perfection in everything
6. Lack of will power

Ways to improve one's self-esteem

If the current performance and behaviour is consistent and at the peak, the self-esteem is said to be high. You remain happy, have more energy and remain positive. Life improves as self-esteem rises. Here, are some ways to increase self-esteem.

1. **Exercise daily.** Look after your body for an hour and it will look after you for

the remaining twenty three hours. It's one thing that has a long-term effect on the mental and physical well-being. An hour of exercises keeps it going all day long. Remind yourself that your self-esteem needs this workout.

2. **Keep your commitments.** Especially the ones you make to yourself. When one does not fulfil the commitments made to himself and others he ends up being dissatisfied with himself and others.

3. **Plan your work and work your plan.** The paradigm may look old but very much applicable in the present context. When one implements his plan he is up to what he is capable of doing there by causing a high self esteem.

4. **Help someone else.** Do something good others without being asked. Only powerful people do these sorts of things.

5. **Remember your purpose.** Individuals are created to provide a valuable service or resource to the rest of the people in the world. Remembering this fact causes self-esteem to rise.

> The longest journey possible by a person is the journey within.
> –Dr.K.Alex

6. **Act on your purpose.** One should be able to know the purpose of one's life. If not so try he should try to find at the earliest. One should try to one thing a day that suits the purpose of his life. This improves how one feels about his life.

7. **Learn something new.** Learning

something new always makes one feel satisfied. It does not matter if nothing happens. But one feels better about himself for having learned something new. After all, he can have that information the next time he needs it.

8. **Get involved in some sort of teaching.** Teaching others will always make people to learn something. Teaching someone else to do something successfully – meaning that he can then do it for himself. That's why people are always drawn to teachers for they are full of self-esteem.

Take time to laugh.
It is the music of the soul.
Take time to think.
It is the source of power.
Take time to play.
It is the source of perpetual youth.
Take time to read.
It is the fountain of wisdom.
Take time to pray.
It is the greatest power on Earth.
Take time to love and be loved.
It is a God-given privilege.
Take time to be friendly.
It is the road to happiness.
Take time to give.
It is too short a day to be selfish.
Take time to work.
It is the price of success.
-- Anonymous

Books for further reading

- The Managing Change Pocketbook, Jones and Neil .R, Management Pocket Books Ltd, 1995.
- The Self Esteem Companion: Simple Exercises to Help You Challenge Your Inner Critic and Celebrate Your Personal Strengths, Patrick Fanning, Carole Honey church et al, New Harbinger Publications, 1st Oct 2005.
- 10 Simple Solutions for building Self Esteem: How to end Self Doubt, Gain Confidence and Create a Positive Self Image, Glenn R.Schiraldi, 2007.
- Self Esteem: A Proven program of cognitive Technique for assessing, Improving, and Maintaining Your Self Esteem, Matthew McKay, New Harbinger Publications, 2005.
- Getting it done: The Transforming power of Self Discipline, Andrew J Dubrin and Peterson Guides, 1995.
- Managing Intense Emotions and Overcoming Self Destructive Habits: A self Help Manual, Lorraine bell, Bruner Routledge, 2005.
- Successful Self-Management, Revised Edition: Increasing Your Personal Effectiveness, Paul R Timm, Crisp learning Publication Inc, 1993.
- The Power of Self Management: Pride and Professionalism for a Successful Career, Michael Henry Cohen, Creative health Care Management Inc, 2008.
- The Self Managing Environment, Alan Roberts, Rowman and Littlefield, 1980.

2 Managing Others/ Interpersonal Skills

LEARNING OUTCOME

- Introduction
- Stages in interpersonal relationship
- Improving relationship
- Transactional Analysis
- The three ego states
  - Parent:
  - Adult:
  - Child:
- JOHARI WINDOW
- Characters associated with open area
- Characters associated with blind area
- Characters associated with hidden area
- Characters associated with unknown area
- The Ideal Window
- Johari adjectives
- Four Life Positions
- Characters associated with persons in life positions
- Books for further reading

Introduction

> Relationship is talking to each other and not talking about each other.

Interpersonal skills are the skills that people use to interact with other people. It is also referred to as people skills. It involves using skills such as behaving, communicating, listening, and relating with people.

Interpersonal relationship is an association between two or more people that may soon pass by or last for a long period. Generally such relationship is formed based on parent-child relationship, teacher-student relationship, love, solidarity, business interactions and social commitments.

Interpersonal skills essentially mean how people relate to one another. It is often used in business contexts to measure a person's ability to operate in the working environment through his communication and interactions.

> No matter how busy you are, you must take time to make the other person feel important.
>
> -Mary Kay Ash

Positive interpersonal relationship in the work place increases the interdependence of the employees. People with good interpersonal skills tend to influence each other. This interdependence and influence leads to improved performance of the employees. Improved and enhanced interpersonal skills increases the productivity in the organisation since it ensures better understanding and comfortable communication among employees.

Stages in interpersonal relationship

A relationship between individuals is formed in the following ways.

1. **Acquaintance.** People come to know each other on their first meetings and begin to like each other. Their continued relationship leads to the next stage.

2. **Build up.** At this stage people begin to like and trust each other. The need for intimacy grows as the days pass by.

3. **Continuation.** At this stage people move towards a long-term and stable friendship.

4. **Deterioration.** At this stage the relationship built on trust continues and those that are not built on trust and mutual respect tend to deteriorate.

5. **Termination.** At this stage the relationship comes to an end either by death in the case of a healthy relationship or by separation in the case of a broken relationship.

> Never expect people to treat you any better than you treat yourself.
> – Bo Bennett

Improving relationship

It does not matter how hard a person works and how intelligent is he, if he does not know how to relate with people. One's personal and professional life will be of struggle if he cannot connect with the people he is to work. To experience success in one's life, one has to improve his interpersonal relationships. Here are some ways to improve the same.

1. **Be appreciative.** Learn to find the positive things about the people around you. Learn to praise in public and blame in private.
2. **Listen actively.** One of the best ways to respect the persons is to listen to them with attention.

3. **Personal attention to others.** Attend to others personal needs and if need be, lend a helping hand. Spend time with them while facing tough situations.

4. **Make people come together.** Ensure an environment that provides platform for people to come together.

5. **Learn to communicate.** How one speaks is as important as what he speaks. Particularly at times, when one has to convey unpleasant news, he has to be careful in his choice of words.

6. **Avoid/solve conflicts.** When conflicts cannot be avoided, learn to solve them. Learn the art of mediating and bring the parties to the table for negotiation.

7. **Empathise.** Learn to understand the situations from the perspective of others.

8. **Avoid complaining.** Chronic complaining will bring a bad reputation among the co-workers.

> The most basic and powerful way to connect to another person is to listen. Just listen.
>
> - Rachel Naomi Remen

Transactional Analysis

Transactional Analysis known as TA was developed by Eric Berne during 1950s. It is a model of people and relationships. It is based on two notions. The first notion states that each person is made up of three ego states and the second notion is that they are related to each other. Eric Berne developed the ego states to explain how one is made up of and how he relates to others.

- Eric Berne was born in 1910 in Montreal, Canada. His father was a doctor & his mother was an editor.
- His father died at age 38, when Eric was 9.
- Earned an MD in 1935 from McGill Univ .
- Became a US citizen and served in Utah during WWII, practicing group therapy.
- Was denied membership in the Psychoanalytic Institute in 1956.
- This brought about his rejection of psychoanalysis and was a turning point in his life.
- Wrote the book Games People Play
- Died of a heart attack in 1970 at the age of 60.

> The magic words for a great relationship are, "I love you just the way you are.
>
> - Jonathan Lockwood Huie

The three ego states

Eric Berne states that each person is made up of three ego states. They are Parent, Adult and Child. These terms have different definitions than in normal language.

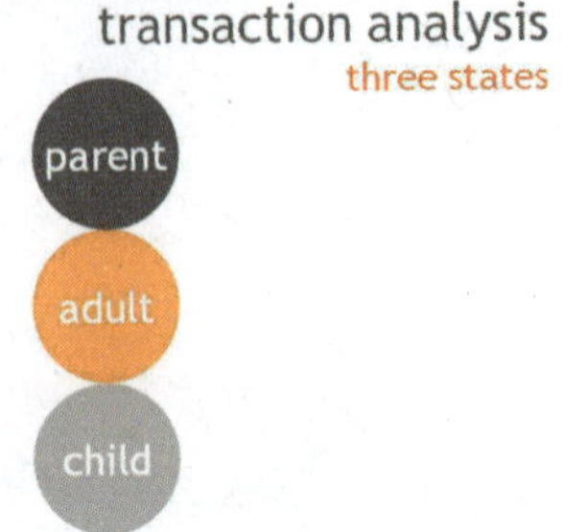

Parent (one's own parents)

This is a set of feelings, thinking and behaving that people copy from their parents, neighbours, teachers, relatives and so on. As a person grows up he takes in ideas, beliefs, values, feelings and behaviour from the above mentioned. People behave in the way they saw them others behaving. This reflects one's voice of authority, attitudes and learning. This stage is formed based on the external events and influences on a person. Studies also reveal that it is not easy to change this stage since formed from childhood.

In short,

Parent: when a person thinks, feels & behaves in ways copied from his/her parents

Adult (a data processing computer)

Adult is one's ability to think and determine action for themselves based the input received. It is a stage about direct responses to the here and now. It is a stage of being spontaneous and aware with the capacity for intimacy. In this stage people see people as they are rather than how they see them. In this stage people ask for information from others rather than making assumptions. If parent stage is taking from the past, this stage is about using the past experiences appropriately.

In short,

Adult: thoughts, feelings, or behaviours that are a direct result of current happenings

Child (a little professor)

Child stage is a set of behaviours, thoughts and feelings which are replayed from our childhood. It is the reaction to external events.

In short,

Child: thinking, feeling, behaving as one did as a child

Parent is our 'Taught' concept of life.
Adult is our 'Thought' concept of life.
Child is our 'Felt' concept of life

Transactional Analysis is a language within a language. It is language that tries to give the true meanings for the words spoken and actions exhibited. This helps people to have effective communication and maintain better relationship.

JOHARI WINDOW

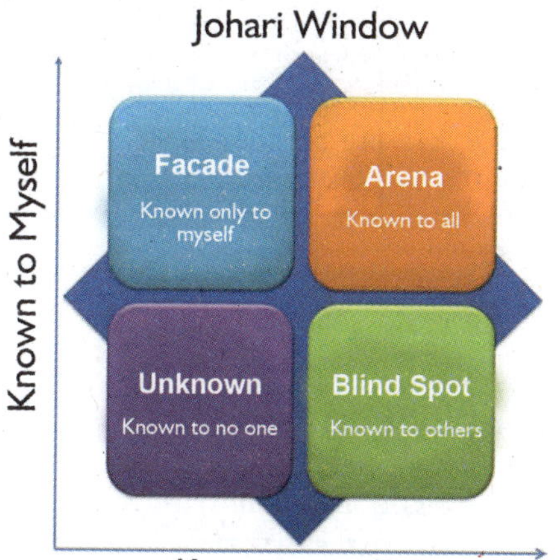

The Johari Window, named after the first names of its inventors, Joseph Luft and Harry Ingham, is a model describing the process of human interaction. It is a tool created to understand people's interpersonal skills and communication.

1 open/free area	2 blind area
3 hidden area	4 unknown area

JOHARI WINDOW

The Johari Window model is referred to as a 'disclosure model of self awareness'. This represents information within or about a person in relation to the group they belong to. A four paned "window," as shown below, divides personal awareness into four different types: open, hidden, blind, and unknown.

Characters associated with open area

The first pane, the open/free area contains things that I know about myself and about which the group knows. This pane increases in size as the level of trust increases between individuals or between an individual and the group. Individuals share more information, particularly personally relevant information.

Characters associated with blind area

The second pane, the blind area contains information that I do not know about myself but of which the group may know. The people in the group learn from my verbal cues, mannerisms, the way I say things, or the style in which I relate to others.

Characters associated with hidden area

Pane three, the hidden area contains information that I know about myself but the group does not know. I keep these things hidden from them.

Characters associated with unknown area

The fourth and last pane, the unknown contains things that neither I nor the group knows about me. I may never become aware of material buried far below the surface in my unconscious area.

The size of the pane can be different depending on the group, team or situation the person is in. In any new situation the open space is likely to be small because shared awareness is relatively less.

As the team members become established and known, the size of the team member's open free area quadrant increases.

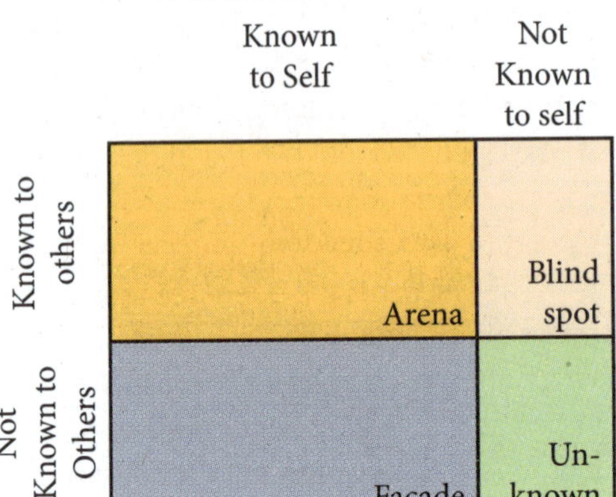

Johari Window

The Ideal Window in the first example reflects a high degree of trust in the group or in any relationship significant to the person. If an individual is in this window, the size of Arena increases because of increased trust level in the group. The norms developed by the group for giving and receiving feedback facilitate this kind of exchange. The large Arena suggests that much of the behaviour is open to the group members. Because of this openness, other group members do not need to interpret (or misinterpret) or project more personal meanings into others behaviour. They understand the actions and words, and they know you are open.

One does not need a large Arena with everyone. Sometimes this kind of openness is seen as threatening or inappropriate because of the relationship you have with them. The more open you are in dealing with others, the fewer games you play in relationships.

Johari adjectives

A Johari window consists of the following 56 adjectives used to describe a person.

able	calm	confident
accepting	caring	dependable
adaptable	cheerful	dignified
bold	clever	energetic
brave	complex	extroverted
friendly	mature	self-assertive
giving	modest	self-conscious
happy	nervous	sensible
helpful	observant	sentimental
idealistic	organized	shy
independent	patient	silly
ingenious	powerful	smart
intelligent	proud	spontaneous
introverted	quiet	sympathetic
kind	reflective	tense
knowledgeable	relaxed	trustworthy
logical	religious	warm
loving	responsive	wise
	searching	witty

Count your age not by years but by friends.

Four Life Positions

You are okay with me

I am not okay with me			I am okay with me
	I am not ok **You are ok** **one down position** **Get away from** **Helpless**	**I am ok** **You are ok** **Healthy position** **Get on with** **Happy**	
	I am not ok **You are not ok** **Hopeless position** **Get nowhere** **with Hopeless**	**I am ok** **You are not ok** **One-up position** **Get rid of** **Angry**	

You are not okay with me

Life positions works with the assumption that people choose very early on in their life (before age 2). It represents the fundamental stance a person takes about him and other people. Once a child has taken up a favorite position, he is likely to construct his view to match that life position. In other words it works with a basic stance towards self and other people.

One's life position is like a set of glasses through which we see the world. If one is going to see through a yellow colour glass the world is going to look yellow and seeing through the green colour glass will show the world green. The world looks different not because of the world but due to the glass through which one sees the world.

The phrase I'm OK, You're OK is one of four "life positions" that each of us may take. The four positions are:

1. I'm Not OK, You're OK
2. I'm Not OK, You're Not OK
3. I'm OK, You're Not OK
4. I'm OK, You're OK

I "'I am ok, you are ok," means "I am ok with myself and with you too."

2. "I am ok, you are not ok," means "I am ok with myself but not with you. I feel there is something wrong with other people around me."

3. "I am not ok, you are ok," means "There is something fundamentally wrong with me, but everybody else is ok."

4. "I am not ok, you are not ok," means "There is something fundamentally wrong with me as well as other people."

I am not ok, you are ok	**I am ok, you are ok**
Depressive Position	Good Life Position
I am not ok, you are not ok	**I am ok, you are not ok**
Futile Position	Paranoid Position

Characters associated with persons in life positions

I am O.K; You are O.K

- High emotional intelligence
- Express confidence in self
- Trust in others

I am O.K; You are not O.K

- Attitude-'i am always right'
- Generally operates from high critical parent and rebellious child ego states

- Highly prescriptive any disagreement arouses a strong reaction.

I am not O.K; You are O.K

- Quite submissive
- Less innovative
- Lacks risk taking responsibilities
- Operates mostly from compliant child ego

I am not O.K; You are not O.K

- Most destructive life position
- Very low 'adult ego' state and other ego states are also not functionally distributed
- Helpless, depressed, miserable, suicidal
- lack of confidence
- Do not trust others

Books for further reading

- How To Manage People Effectively, Emilia Gallo, Inkstone Books, June 5, 2007.
- The Art of Managing People, Tony Alessandra and Phillip L. Hunsaker, Dorling Kindersley, June 1, 2009.
- Managing People Effectively (First Time Manager), Jean Civil, Cassell Illustrated, 1997.
- Managing People, Jane Weightman, CIPD house, 2004.
- How to Successfully Manage People, Jon Anshutz, Jon Publication, July 29, 2006.
- Managing People and Organizations in Changing Contexts, Graeme Martin, A Butterworth-Heinemann Title, 16 Mar 2006.
- Organizational Behavior: Managing People and Organizations, Ricky W. Griffin and Gregory Moorhead, Cengage Learning, 12-Jan-2009.
- Managing People: A Practical Guide, Byron Lane and Richard Rierdan, softcover, 2001.
- Managing people and Processes, Dr. John A. Kline, Armed forces Comptroller, 2008.
- The Everything Managing People Book: Quick And Easy Ways to Build, Motivate, And Nurture a First-rate Team (Everything (Business & Personal Finance), Gary R. McClain, Deborah S. Romaine, Adams Media Corpora, December 18, 2008.
- The New Art of Managing People, Updated and Revised: Person-to-Person Skills, Guidelines, and Techniques Every Manager Needs to Guide, Direct, and Motivate the Team, Tony Alessandra and Phillip L Hunsaker, Free Press, July 17, 1986.
- If Managing People Were Easy... Everyone Would Do It!, Gina Abudi, Abudi consulting group, 2012

Managing Your Time

LEARNING OUTCOME

- The 80:20 rule
- Take a good look at the people around you
- Examine your work
- Sense of time management
- Time is money
- Features of time
- Three secrets of time management
- Time management matrix
- Analysis of time matrix
- Effective scheduling
- Grouping of activities
- Five steps to successful time management
- Difficulties in time management
- Evils of not planning
- Time management is a myth
- Overcoming procrastination ways to find free time
- Time management tips for students
- Interesting facts about time
- Ideal way of spending a day
- Time wasters
- Time savers
- Realizing the value of time
- Time circle planner
- Exercise : Test your time management skills

"The busy man has time for everything".

Introduction

You can't add any more hours to your day so learning to manage your time more effectively will help you plan your work more efficiently and ensure deadlines are met. Managing time effectively is a particularly crucial ingredient in successful projects. It is important to manage both your personal and professional lives because as much as you try to keep them separate they cannot help but infringe upon one another. Managing your own time will not only benefit you but those around you as well.

The busy man only can manage to do many things, which seem to be beyond the reach of ordinary persons. The life of great leaders teaches us one lesson. They have to do many things in spite of their busy schedule. The secret therefore lies in scientific management of time.

When a person says that he has no time, what he really means is that he is unable to manage his time properly. The idea of time management has been in existence for more than 100 years.

The term time management should not be misunderstood as time can be managed. In fact time can't be managed. By time management what we mean is we need to manage ourselves according to the time.

Time management is actually self-management. The skills that we need to mange others are the same skills that are required to manage ourselves. Namely, the ability to plan, organize, direct and control.

The 80:20 rule

Reference is made to the 80:20 rule of time management, which is rooted in what is known as the Pareto Principle.

Vilfredo Pareto, an Italian economist, discovered this principle in 1897 when he observed that 80 percent of the land in England (and every country he subsequently studied) was owned by 20 percent of the population. Pareto's theory of predictable imbalance has since been applied to almost every aspect of modern life.

The 80:20 rule states that the relationship between input and output is rarely, balanced. When applied to work, it means that approximately 20 percent of your efforts produce 80 percent of the results. Learning to recognize and then focus on that 20 percent is the key to making the most effective use of your time. Here are two quick tips to develop 80/20 thinking.

According to Pareto Principle, or the 80:20 rule, 80% of unfocussed effort generates 20% of the results. The remaining 80% of results are achieved with only 20% of the effort.

Take a good look at the people around you

Twenty percent of your colleagues, staff and friends probably give you 80 percent of the support and satisfaction you need. They are your true advocates. Take good care of them. Likewise, you can probably name several friends and family members who would be there for you under any circumstances.

Examine your work

Ask yourself, "What do I really want to do with my life and my time? What 20 percent of my work should I be focusing on?"

Here are some signs that will help you to recognize whether you're spending your time as you should:

You're in your 80 percent if:

- You're working on tasks other people want you to, but you have no investment in them.
- You're frequently working on tasks labelled "urgent."
- You're spending time on tasks you are not usually good at doing.
- Activities are taking a lot longer than you expected.
- You find yourself complaining all the time.

You're in your 20 percent if:

- You're engaged in activities that advance your overall purpose in life.
- You're doing things you have always wanted to do or that makes you feel good about yourself.
- You're working on tasks you don't like, but you're doing them knowing they relate to some advantages.
- You're hiring people to do the tasks you are not good at or don't like doing.
- You're smiling.

Sense of time management

Several years ago a foreign clock manufacturer who visited India with a view to setting up an alarm clock factory returned to his country giving up his idea. He said that there was not enough time consciousness in India as yet to justify manufacture of alarm clocks for another 20 years. This comment hurts our national pride, but it is a fact. It is high time we develop time consciousness.

Time is money

Man, machine, method and materials are considered to be an investment. But today in the contest of globalization, time is also considered as one of the prime investment factor. In terms of day-to-day economic life, time is simply money. Every delay eventually means loss of money.

> "Time is like an arrow, once it leaves the bow, it does not come back".

Features of time

1. Time is an asset. It is an asset of fictitious nature.
2. Time is an opportunity. It is a chance given to an individual to create, innovate and manufacture something.
3. Supply is limited. Time is limited in its supply.

> "Time is very democratic in nature because it treats all persons absolutely impartially".

Three secrets of time management

1. **Value of time.** Unlike money and material, time once lost cannot be regained or replaced. Besides, time is a resource which cannot be substituted.

2. **Time budgeting.** More than money, time is to be budgeted properly.

3. **Concentration**. Concentration is doing one's immediate duty on hand with proper care and attention. Such care and attention is possible only when a person has concentration in what he does.

Time management matrix

Urgent	Not Urgent	
Important	1. Do now	2. Plan to do
Not important	3. Reject and explain	4. Resist and cease

1. Do now

- Emergencies
- Crisis
- Demands from the boss
- Planned tasks due now
- Seeing a doctor when sick
- Seeing the days news
- Meetings and appointments
- Paying phone bills

2. Plan to do

- Studying
- Panning
- Relationship building
- Developing changes
- Replying important letters
- Eating regularly healthy food
- Attending classes
- Taking up revision tests

3. Reject and explain

- Attending some phone calls
- Attending parties
- Seeing a movie
- Taking account of attractive discount sales
- Trivial request from others
- Adhoc interruptions/ distraction
- Apparent emergences
- Pointless routine activities

4. Resist and cease

- Watching movies
- Watching TV
- Chatting with friends
- Internet chatting
- Sight seeing
- Shopping\computer games
- Day dreaming

"Do not postpone to tomorrow what can be finished today".

Analysis of time matrix

Is the task important or not?

❖ Important tasks are those that are essential for achieving your goals and living a meaningful life. Sharing time with your family, professional development and training, socializing, being active and healthy, may be important to your personal and professional goals. Activities that contribute to your vision and goals exist in quadrant 1 or 2.

❖ On the other hand, spending time on routine e-mails and phone calls, attending some meetings, watching TV, may not be so important to your personal and professional goals.

- Urgent tasks are those that cannot be put off. Phone calls and snap deadlines from your boss are things that you can't really put off. The reality is that things will pop up unannounced that will demand your immediate attention.
- Non-urgent tasks are those things that don't demand our immediate attention. They may include making some types of phone calls, watching TV, some forms of socializing, planning your time, setting goals.
- These activities reside in quadrants 3 or 4 of the time management matrix.

Remaining in Quadrant 2

- From a time management point of view, we want to spend most of our time in quadrant 2, proactively pursuing those things that are important to us.
- What activities do you do that fall into quadrant 2? These are tasks that are important but not urgent. Activities that typically fall into quadrant 2 of the time management matrix are prevention-related activities, computer maintenance; relationship building; strategic planning, training and goal setting; recognizing new opportunities and vacations.
- By doing these important tasks in quadrant 2 of the time management matrix, we are able to devote the time that is needed before they become urgent. However, often urgent things crowd out the important things – it is easy to happen and results in stress and ineffective use of our time.

Moving from Quadrant 2 to Quadrant 1

From a time management point of view, if you are spending most of your time in quadrant 1 it implies that you are a poor planner and sooner or later you will experience stress.

What activities do you do that fall into quadrant 1? Typically these tasks are done because they are urgent, and their importance means they have to be done. This is a stressful use of your time.

Being in quadrant 1 is stressful. There are some important things that are best done in a proactive way (in quadrant 2), but if you don't attend to these things, then these important things become urgent and may turn out to be crises (quadrant 1).

Quadrant 3

This is an urgent but unimportant task. What activities do you do that fall into quadrant 3? These may be tasks that land on your desk, or an unimportant phone call.

You will find that there are many tasks that fall into Quadrant 3 for you, and it is a good idea to examine whether the tasks have to be done, as more benefit will come from spending time on those things that move you towards your goals.

Quadrant 4

This type of task is not urgent and not important. These tasks do not move you towards your goals, and could be dropped, so that you can do more value-added tasks. What activities do you do that fall into quadrant 4?

- People in quadrant 3 and 4 waste lot of time
- More time spent in quadrant 3 and 4 will expand quadrant 1
- People in quadrant 3 and 4 struggle to meet dead lines
- Giving more weightage to quadrant 2 will make quadrant 1 shrink automatically.

My interest is in the future, because I am going to spend the rest of my life there.

Effective scheduling

Scheduling is the process by which you look at the time available to you and plan how you will use it to achieve the goals you have set.

A schedule is a tool that helps you plan your time and work. Think of it as a time map with every task spread out in plain sight. You are in control. You can move the tasks around and change the amount of time you wish to allot. When the schedule is finally set up, it will work well since everything is planned and accounted for the way you want it to be.

Many people see schedules as an inflexible method of organizing time. An inflexible schedule, however, is both useless and destructive. Instead, create a schedule to suit your individual needs and personality, one which will help you study at the best possible time.

Since it is your schedule, you can decide how flexible or rigid the schedule needs to be to get tasks done. An effective schedule reflects your personality. Match your personality with your schedule.

Study Time - how much time should you allot for studying and how should it be distributed? In general, plan on two to three hours of study per week for every academic unit. However, if you're spending more than four hours per unit, you may be studying ineffectively. Only you can determine how much time you need.

> "Time is the scarcest resource of the manager; If it is not managed, nothing else can be managed".
>
> *Peter F Drucker, (1909-2005), Management Guru*

Scheduling helps in

- Understanding what you can really achieve
- Making the best use of time available
- Leaving enough time for things that you absolutely must do
- Preserving contingency time to handle the unexpected
- Minimizing stress

Grouping of activities

The activities that you carry out in a day can be grouped into two categories

★ **Maintenance tasks** – These are the activities that ensure you survive. They are sleeping, driving, standing in line, eating, open mail, dressing and grooming

★ **Improvement tasks** – These are the activities that ensure you thrive. These activities add value by moving you closer to your long–term ambitions

Spend 80% of your time in improvement tasks and 20% in maintenance task.

Combining the two tasks

✓ If you can combine maintenance and improvement tasks, you are considered good at managing your time

✓ If you have to eat, you can eat with your family members / subordinates to improve relationship

✓ If you have to go to the 3rd floor you can use the elevator and save time

Five steps to successful time management

- Set specific goals (be it academic or personal)
- Create a term calendar recording major events
- Create a weekly schedule of your classes, meeting, etc.
- Decide on specific times to work on each course
- Make a to-do list for each day the night before

Difficulties in time management

Here are some of the most frequent reasons for not being able to manage the time sensibly. These reasons are also called time stealers.

- Interruptions – telephone
- Interruptions – visitors
- Meetings
- Indecision
- Acting with incomplete information
- Unclear communication
- Lack of planning
- Inability to say "no

Evils of not planning

- Procrastination (postponing)
- Set-back (failure)
- Confusion
- Inability to act
- Set back to relationship
- Inferiority complex
- Depressed

Time Management is a myth

Time management is a myth. What a big fantasy. You can't manage time. You can only manage yourself according to the time and not vice versa. Every day you receive 24 hours. You can't add more nor do you get any less time. Erase time management from your brain and start thinking out of the clock. Experts are of the opinion that it is not Time Management but is Self Management. You have to organize your activities to fit the clock.

The word time management, because that's how people use it. They think they have a time management problem. In reality it's an activity problem. One of the first things we have to do is to shift their mindset from time management to Self Management.

Overcoming Procrastination

1. Break it Down

Break your tasks down into manageable steps. Break them down into smaller categories.

2. Get Help

If you can't find a way to follow through, take the help of someone who can. You can either take the help of your family members or a friend.

3. Ask "Why"

Ask yourself why are you putting it off? If you can get to the heart of your procrastination, you may be able to find a different reason altogether.

4. Just Skip it

Looking for the cause of your procrastination will benefit you to answer the following questions. "Does it really have to be taken care of right now?" or, "Does it have to be taken care of at all?"

If you've been putting something off time and again, there's a chance it doesn't need to be done at all.

5. Just Do It

If you feel it has to be done, don't waste your precious time worrying or stressing out about it. Just get up and start doing it.

Ways to Find Free Time

"The real problem of leisure time is how to keep others from using yours."

- Arthur Lacey

Everyone has the same amount of time, and it's in great demand. But some have managed to find time to do things that they love and others have allowed the demands, pressures and responsibilities of life to dominate the days.

It's time to move from the second group back into the first. Reclaim your time. Create the life you want and make the most of the free time you have. It's not hard, though it does take a little bit of effort and diligence.

Choose the ones you can apply and give them a try:

1. Take a time out. This starts with taking a step back to take a good look at your life. You need to block off at least an hour. Several hours or half a day is better. A whole day would be awesome. A weekend would be even more ideal. With this block of time, take a look at your life with some perspective. Ask yourself few questions like, Is it what I have always wanted? How would I get to where I have always wanted to be? What do I enjoy doing, but don't have enough time to do? What things actually fill up my day? Are there things I could drop or minimize to make more time?

2. Find your essentials. What is it that you love to do? Make a short list of 4-5 things. These are the things you want to make room for.

3. Find your time-wasters. Where do you spend a lot of your time? Take a close look at these things and really think about whether they're necessary? Find out if there are ways to reduce, minimize or eliminate these things.

4. Schedule the time. Take time to find out what you wanted to do and what you actually did. Find out the deviation and ensure that it is not alarming.

5. Consolidate. There are many things you do throughout your day or your week. You need to consolidate in order to save time. For example instead of doing a work one or two a day, do them all in one day to save time and energy.

6. Cut out meetings. You can, minimize the number of meetings you hold and attend.

After all Warren Buffet holds meeting only twice a year with his subordinates.

7. Schedule your schedule. If you have a heavily packed schedule, full of meetings, assignments, projects and appointments, you have to weed it out so that it's not so jam-packed. Find the stuff that's not so essential and cancel them.

8. Re-think your routine. Often we get stuck with our routine. We need to find a way out to make the day interesting. Is there a better way of doing things? You're the creator of your life make a new routine that's more pleasant, more optimal, more filled with things you love.

9. Cut back on email. How often do you check email? How much time do you spend composing emails? If you spend a major part of your work day on email, as many people do, you are bound to run in short of time

10. Learn to say no. If you say "yes" to every request, you will never have any free time. Learn to say "no" to everything except the essential requests.

11. Keep your list to 3. When you prepare your daily to-do list, ensure that you list as many as only three Most Important Tasks you want to accomplish today. By keeping your task list small, you ensure that you are getting the important work done at same time not overloading yourself.

12. Do your important task first. Of the three Most Important Tasks you choose for the day, pick the biggest one, or the one you're dreading most, and do that first. Don't allow yourself to be engaged in tiny tasks until you finish the important one. It starts your day with a sense of major accomplishment, and leaves you with a lot of free time the rest of the day, because the most important thing is already done.

13. Delegate. You don't need to do everything yourself. If necessary, spend a little time training the person to whom you're delegating the task, but that little time spent training will pay off in a lot of time saved later. Delegating allows you to focus on the core tasks and projects you should be focusing on.

14. Cut out distractions. Identify the distracters around your workspace that distract you from the task at hand and try to eliminate/avoid them. The distracters could be the papers lying around that call for your attention and action, email, the phone, or coworkers.

15. Disconnect. The biggest of distractions, for most people, is the Internet. If you really want to be able to effectively complete tasks, disconnect your Internet so you can really focus. Set certain times of the day for connectivity, and only connect during those periods.

16. Outsource. If you can't delegate, see if you can outsource. With the Internet, we can connect with people from all over. You can outsource many things, from small tasks to checking email to legal work to design and editing work and more. That allows you to focus on the things you are best at, the things you love doing, and saves you a lot of time.

17. Make use of your mornings. Mornings are the absolute best times to schedule the things you want to do. Mornings are great because your day hasn't been filled with unscheduled tasks. Schedule your tasks in the morning, and it'll rarely get pushed back.

18. The work after work Time. Other than mornings, the time just after work is very useful for doing Essential things. Exercise, pursuing the hobbies, going through magazines, and so on can be done after the work time.

19. Your evenings. The time before you go to bed is also very important, as it exists every single day, and it's usually completely yours to schedule. Spend time with your family members, the kids, their studies, homework could all be done during this time.

20. Lunch breaks. Lunch breaks are another good opportunity to schedule things. Some people like to exercise, or to take quiet times, during their lunch breaks. Others use this time to work on an important personal goal or project.

Time management tips for students

Here are some tips to help you get more out of every day, both your school/college day and during your personal time. These tips can increase your success and help you to have more fun along the way.

1. Plan an hour per day for "Me Time". Give twenty-three hours to school/ colleges, your friends, and your family but keep one hour for yourself.

During this hour add a new dimension to your life. Read books, learn a hobby, learn a foreign language, develop computer skills, start a business, spend time on health development etc. By taking one hour per day of focused study, any of you can become a world-class expert in a topic of our choice.

2. Establish a regular reading program. It can be just fifteen minutes a day. With that small investment of time, the average person will read fifteen books in a year. Also, consider taking a Speed Reading course. It will help you to double your reading rate and comprehension. You can read what you have to read in half the time.

3. Overload your days. Create a daily action plan that includes not only the things you "have to do", but the things you "want to do". If you give yourself one thing to do during the day, it will take you all day. If you give yourself two things to do during the day, you get them both done. If you give yourself twelve things to do, you may not get twelve done, but you may get eight done.

Having a lot to do in a day creates a healthy sense of pressure on you to get focused and get it done.

4. Prioritize your list of "things to do". Some of your tasks are "crucial" and some of your tasks are "not crucial". You have a tendency to get attracted to the "not crucial" items because they are typically quicker, more fun, and easier to do. Identify the most important task you need to do. You may not get everything done but you will get the most important things done.

5. Radiate a genuine, positive attitude. When you are in a negative mood you tend to annoy the positive people who do not want to be brought down by your negativity. This includes your friends, your family, and your teachers. And, when you are in a negative mood, you have a natural system set up to attract the other negative people to you. Positive people help to bring you up. Negative people help to bring you down.

Interesting facts about time

An average Indian lives for 60 years. Here is how he spends his 60 years

Activities	Time spent
Waiting at signals	6 months
Looking for misplaced objects	1.0 Year
Driving a two wheeler	2.5 Years
Waiting in queue	5.0 Years
Eating	6.0 Years
In bathroom	7.0 Years
In workplace	15.0 Years
In bed	23.0 Years
Total	60.0 years

Ideal way of spending a day

- 45% of each day meeting biological needs (sleeping, dressing, grooming, eating)
- 40% of each day at work
- 15% of each day socializing

It takes time to save time

Here is how Mr. X spends his time		Here is how Mr. X. should spend his time	
Activities	**Hours spent**	**Activities**	**Hours spent**
Sleep	10 hrs	Sleep	8 hrs
Eating	2 hrs	Eating	1½ hrs
Socializing	3 hrs	Socializing	1 hr
Personal	3 hrs	Personal	2 hrs
Travel	1 hr	Travel	1 hr
Classes	4 hrs	Classes	4 hrs
Reading	1 hr	Reading	3½ hrs
Writing	0 hr	Writing	1 hr
Thinking	0 hr	Thinking	1 hr
Exercising	0 hr	Exercising	1 hr

Time wasters

- Indecision
- Inefficiency
- Unanticipated interruptions that do not pay off
- Procrastination
- Unrealistic time estimates
- Unnecessary errors
- Crisis Management
- Poor organization
- Ineffective meetings
- Micro-management
- Doing urgent rather than important things
- Poor planning and lack of contingency plans
- Failure to delegate or delegating without authority
- Lack of priorities, standards, policies or procedures

Time savers

- Manage the decision making process; not the decisions
- Concentrate on doing only one task at a time
- Establish daily, short-term, mid-term and long-term goals
- Handle correspondence quickly with short letters or memos
- Throw unneeded things away
- Establish personal deadlines and ones for your organization
- Do not waste other people's time
- Ensure all meetings have a purpose, a time limit, and include only essential people

- Get rid of busy work
- Maintain accurate calendars and abide by them
- Know when to stop a task, policy or procedure
- Delegate everything possible and empower subordinates
- Keep things simple
- Ensure time is set aside for high priority tasks
- Set aside time for reflection
- Use checklists and to do lists
- Adjust priorities as a result of new tasks

Realizing the value of time

- To realize the value of **ONE YEAR**,
  Ask a student who failed a grade.
- To realize the value of **ONE MONTH**,
  Ask a mother who gave birth to a premature boy.
- To realize the value of **ONE WEEK**,
  Ask the editor of a weekly newspaper.
- To realize the value of **ONE HOUR**,
  Ask the lovers who are waiting to meet.
- To realize the value of **ONE MINUTE**,
  Ask a person who missed the train.
- To realize the value of **ONE SECOND**,
  Ask a person who just avoided an accident.
- To realize the value of **ONE MILLISECOND**,
  Ask the person who won a silver medal in the Olympics.

Time circle planner

Using different colours or symbols for each type of activity, you can fill up the time circle planner given below. By doing this exercise you can find out which activities take up too much time and the one left out or don't receive sufficient time.

Ineffective time management is a key source of stress.

How do you use your time?

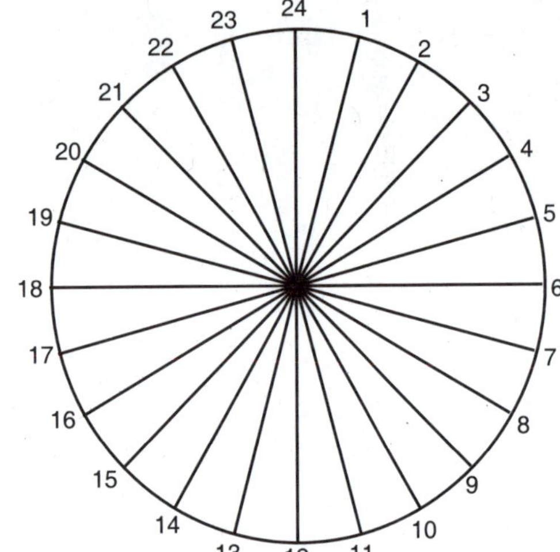

How do you want to use your time?

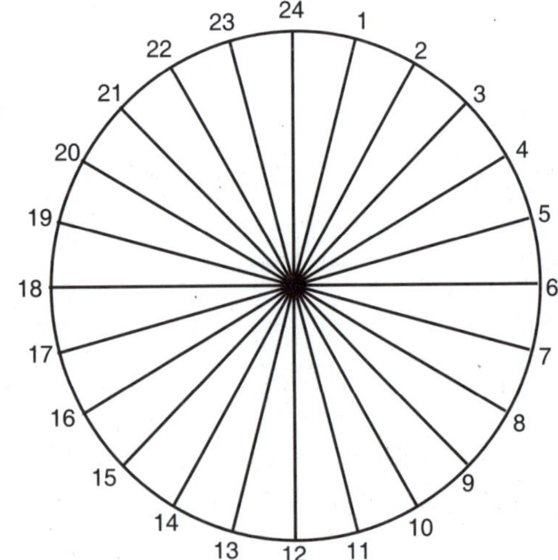

Exercise

Test Your Time Management Skills

Instructions

Rate each question on a scale of 1 to 10. (1 is never. 10 is always. 5 is sometimes. Be specific. Try not to answer 5)

1. Do I ever postpone decisions?
   1 2 3 4 5 6 7 8 9 10
2. Do I ever procrastinate?
   1 2 3 4 5 6 7 8 9 10
3. Do I put off my routine work?
   (Washing, cleaning, writing letters etc.)
   1 2 3 4 5 6 7 8 9 10
4. Do I get buried with reading?
   1 2 3 4 5 6 7 8 9 10
5. Do I have too many interruptions during work/study?
   1 2 3 4 5 6 7 8 9 10
6. Do I put off difficult tasks because they need hard work?
   1 2 3 4 5 6 7 8 9 10
7. Do I fail to delegate and share my work with others with whom I work?
   1 2 3 4 5 6 7 8 9 10
8. Do I have too many visitors?
   1 2 3 4 5 6 7 8 9 10
9. Do I have trouble saying no?
   1 2 3 4 5 6 7 8 9 10
10. Do I attempt too much at once?
    1 2 3 4 5 6 7 8 9 10
11. Do I arrive late for meetings, appointments, classes?
    1 2 3 4 5 6 7 8 9 10
12. Do I leave jobs undone?
    1 2 3 4 5 6 7 8 9 10
13. Do I leave jobs half done?
    1 2 3 4 5 6 7 8 9 10
14. Do I have a messy stacked study/workarea?
    1 2 3 4 5 6 7 8 9 10
15. Do I always want to do it myself?
    1 2 3 4 5 6 7 8 9 10
16. Do I socialize too much?
    1 2 3 4 5 6 7 8 9 10
17. Do I spend too much time for movies watching TV, reading novels?
    1 2 3 4 5 6 7 8 9 10
18. Do I feel a lack of self discipline?
    1 2 3 4 5 6 7 8 9 10
19. Do I worry a lot about my work/study?
    1 2 3 4 5 6 7 8 9 10
20. Do I feel as though I'm neglecting my family/friends?
    1 2 3 4 5 6 7 8 9 10
21. Do I feel as though I'm not making enough personal contact?

1 2 3 4 5 6 7 8 9 10

22. Do I accept more work than I can handle?

1 2 3 4 5 6 7 8 9 10

23. Do I plan my work/study?

1 2 3 4 5 6 7 8 9 10

24. Do I spend too much time day-dreaming?

1 2 3 4 5 6 7 8 9 10

25. Do I often just hang around doing nothing?

1 2 3 4 5 6 7 8 9 10

Scoring

How many of these questions you have rated 7 or higher? This score will help you to get in touch with the amount of time you might be wasting.

If the majority of your score fall between

- 0 to 8 : You are in great shape. You should have written a book on time management
- 9 to 15 : Right in the middle. Time management will probably help you.
- 16 to 26 : You need help. Not just time management, but probably an appointment secretary too.

Books for further Reading

- Out of Time
- How the Sixteen Types Manage Their Time and Work- Larry Demarest
- Procrastination
- Using Psychological Type Concepts to Help Students Judith A. Provost
- Time Management for Unmanageable People
- The Guilt Free Way to Organize, Energize, and Maximize Your Life Ann McGee-Cooper, Duane Trammell
- Achieving Objectives Made Easy! Practical goal setting tools & proven time management techniques by Raymond Le Blanc
- The 7 Habits of Highly Effective People (Covey) by Stephen R. Covey
- Awaken the Giant Within by Anthony Robbins
- What Matters Most : The Power of Living Your Values by Hyrum W. Smith
- Getting Things Done: The Art of Stress-Free Productivity by David Allen
- How to Get Control of Your Time and Your Life (Signet) by Alan Lakein
- The 25 Best Time Management Tools & Techniques: How to Get More Done Without Driving Yourself Crazy by Pamela Dodd
- The 80/20 Principle: The Secret to Success by Achieving More with Less by Richard Koch
- The 4-Hour Workweek: Escape 9-5, Live Anywhere, and Join the New Rich by Timothy Ferriss
- Help Yourself Get Everything Done : and Still Have Time to Play by Mark Forster
- The Time Trap: The Classic Book on Time Management (Paperback) by Alec Mackenzie (Author) "I just didn't have enough time..." (more
- The Time Trap: The Classic Book on Time Management by Alec Mackenzie (Paperback - Sep 17, 1997)
- Managing Your Time: Practical Guidelines on the Effective Use of Time by Ted W. Engstrom and R. Alec Mackenzie (Mass Market Paperback - 1967)
- Managing Your Time: Practical Guidelines on the Effective Use of Time by Ted

W. Engstrom and R. Alec MacKenzie (Paperback - Jul 1987)

- The Management Process in 3-D by R. Alec Mackenzie (Digital - Jan 5, 2008) - Download: PDF
- Time for Success: A Goal-Getter's Strategy by Alec MacKenzie (Paperback - Jul 1991)
- Managing Your Goals/Audio Cassettes and Workbook by Alec MacKenzie and Mel MacKenzie Brown (Audio Cassette - Jun 1991)
- The horseplayer's guide to winning systems by Alec Mackenzie (Unknown Binding - 1976)
- Teamwork Through Time Management by R. Alec MacKenzie (Paperback - May 1991)
- About Time! a Woman's Guide to Time Management by Alec and Waldo, Kay Cronkite Mackenzie (Paperback - 1981)
- About Time!: A Woman's Guide to Time Management by R. Alec MacKenzie (Paperback - April 1981)
- Alec Mackenzie on Time: "I Guarantee to Increase Your Personal Effectiveness and Improve Your Job Performance by Alec MacKenzie (Hardcover - Feb 1989)
- The Credibility Gap in Management by Chares D.; Mackenzie, R. Alec Flory (Hardcover - 1971)

Strategic Thinking

LEARNING OUTCOME

- Introduction
- Stages in Strategic Thinking
- Areas of application/scope of strategic thinking
- Process of strategic thinking
- Competencies required for strategic thinking
- Importance of strategic thinking
- Characteristics of strategic thinkers
- Developing strategic thinking
- Books for further reading

> Strategic thinking is the bridge that links where you are to where you want to be." -
> John Maxwell

Introduction

Strategic Thinking is an innovative way of thinking regularly about the overall goals of one's job, team, and organization. It is a disciplined thinking with a focus on the desired outcomes of one's personal and professional life.

Strategic thinking emphasises on finding and developing unique opportunities to create value among people who affect a company's direction. Strategic thinking is a way of understanding the fundamental drivers of a business by challenging conventional thinking.

Stages in Strategic Thinking

To achieve results it is important that each stage is well thought out. It is also important is that the stages are completed in an open environment that encourages learning and new ideas.

1. Stage I: Where do you want to be?

Be clear with your vision, mission and objectives.

2. Stage II: How will you know when you get there?

Establish a connection between what is delivered to the customers and what is their expectation through a feedback system.

3. Stage III: Where are you now?

Analyse your strength and weakness to know where you stand in the present day situation. Beware of your today's issues and problem.

4. Stage IV: How do you get there?

This is filling the gap between where are you now and where do you want to go in the future.

5. Stage V: Ongoing:

This implies the strategies as to what should you do to maintain your position you are holding at the moment and position that you would like to hold in the future.

Areas of application/scope of strategic thinking

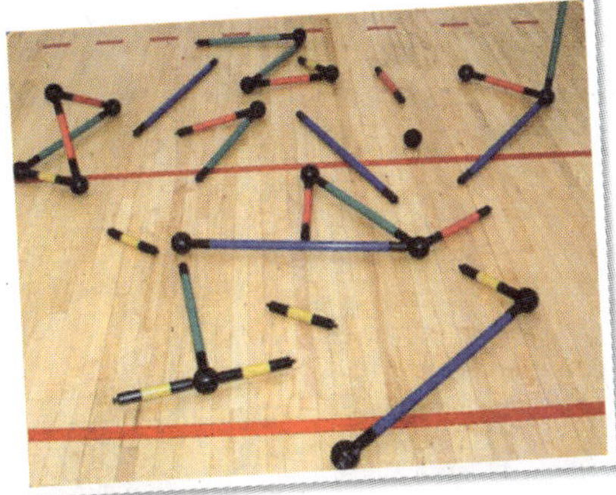

1. Competencies and Skills:

Strategic thinking can be applied by taking into account the company's strength, the competitive edge and its weaknesses.

2. Products and Offerings:

Application of strategic thinking depends on

the products offered, services rendered, the prices prevailing in the market and the image of the company as a whole.

3. Environment and Industry:

Strategic thinking is applied depending on the economic context in which the company is right now in, the kind of government and its policies, the structure of the industry and how the company connects with its customers.

4. Markets and Customers:

Factors like the target customers, their needs, and preparedness of the company in meeting these requirements decide the area of application of strategic thinking.

5. Competitors and Substitutes:

Application of strategic thinking depends on the nature of competition in the industry, the offers made by the competitors, and the counter strategies adopted by them.

6. Suppliers and Buyers:

The application of strategic thinking also depends on the companies one has to work with, their strength and weaknesses and the relative power compared to one's business.

Process of strategic thinking

1. Aligned:

A company's strategies must fit with its vision, mission, objectives, competitive situation and operating strengths.

2. Goal-oriented:

Strategies are the means by which a company sets out to achieve its goals. Hence the strategies should be goal oriented.

3. Fact-based:

The strategies should be based on and supported by real data. Strategic thinking by its very nature is based on assumptions about the future, but these assumptions must be based on educated guesses.

4. Based on Broad Thinking:

Companies that are strategically quick and strong should consider multiple alternatives at a given situation.

5. Focused:

Companies adopting strategic thinking should be clear with what the company wants and does not want. The companies are expected to prioritise the plans and act accordingly.

6. Agreed upon:

While adopting various strategies the company has to ensure that the stakeholders are taken into confidence and aim at getting their fullest support and cooperation.

7. Engaging:

While drafting strategies ensure that the people are educated about the programmes and ensure that the resources are available to them to implement the plans.

8. Adaptable:

Strategies should designed to be adjusted based on the results, experimentation, errors and new information available.

> Only those who can see the invisible, can accomplish the impossible! Patrick Snow

1. a systems perspective

In order to implement strategic thinking, the people concerned should understand the system as a whole and its implication. A complete understanding of end-to-end system, the role within and the skills that are required.

2. Focused

While implementing strategic thinking, there must be more focus and determination than one's rivals. Focus helps in leveraging one's energy and resist distraction.

3. Timely

Thinking in time will help in understanding past, present and future. Such understanding helps in making better and quick decisions.

4. Being creative as well as critical

A strategic thinking should ensure creative as well as critical thinking because it leads to establishing a scientific method.

5. Prudent opportunism

This refers to being open to good opportunities and avenues. Strategies must be developed to suit a changing environment.

> The best way to predict the future is to create it.

Importance of strategic thinking

- Drafting a course of action for the groups
- Making smart long-term decisions
- Gaining the employees' commitment to support the decisions.
- Enhances group's performance and maximize business results.
- Fosters a culture that supports fresh thinking and embraces strategic initiative
- Save time and effort
- Make the most of limited resources
- Attract funding
- Get people on board
- Enhance chances of success
- Increase job satisfaction
- Try to take over the world!

> "No problem can withstand the assault of sustained thinking."
> – Voltaire

Characteristics of strategic thinkers

Strategic thinking necessarily involves certain specific traits, behaviour, attitude and thinking. The following are generally associated with strategic thinkers.

- **Curiosity:** these are the people who are genuinely interested in what is going on in the business.
- **Flexibility:** these are the people who are able to adapt approaches and shift ideas when new information suggests the need to do so.
- **Future focus:** these are the people who constantly consider how the conditions in which the business operates change in the coming days, months and years.
- **Positive outlook:** these are the people who view challenges as opportunities, and believe that success is possible.
- **Openness:** these are the people who welcome new ideas from supervisors, peers, employees, and outside stakeholders such as customers, suppliers, and business partners.

- Breadth: these are the people who continually work to broaden the knowledge and experience, so that they can see connections and patterns among unrelated fields of knowledge.
- A good strategy shortens the road to the goal

– Orison Swett Marden

Developing strategic thinking

1. Have a vision

One should be clear with where he wants to go. If the destination is clear reaching it shouldn't be a problem.

2. Make time

In a busy businesses, making the time is vital. Make time for both thinking and relaxing. Set aside sufficient time both for planning and entertainment as they are equally important.

3. Not being haste

One needs to keep track of the future at the same time he need not to be on a hasted. One needs to carefully design the tomorrows by taking sufficient time.

4. Absorb

In any business it is the question of remaining awake and aware. Every business gives everyone sufficient clues as to what is in store for tomorrow. Of course those clues are often subtle and hidden. Those who are aware and awake are the ones to notice them.

5. Review often

Smart thinkers always check and validate their plans. Plans that are not reviewed often run into difficulties.

6. Learn from Experience

It is said whenever you fail don't fail to take the lessons. A smart thinker uses his experience to think better on vital issues.

7. Use a Team

Two minds put together achieve more. By utilising others one gets not only great ideas but also a great deal of involvement by the members.

8. Be Realistic

One has to be clear with what is achievable given the strengths of the business. Being realistic does not mean holding back but to deliver success.

9. Have check posts

It is always good to create check posts so that one has a chance to change if needed. Check posts helps in spotting the twists.

10. Don't write off

One should not jump to any conclusion when things go wrong because successful future is not bounded by judging their thinking.

Books for further reading

- Thinking Strategically, Avinash K. Dixit et al, W. W. Norton & Company, and April 17, 1993.
- Learning to Think Strategically (New Frontiers in Learning), Julia Sloan, Butterworth-Heinemann, June 15, 2006.
- Strategic Thinking: A Four Piece Puzzle, Bill Birnbaum, Douglas Mountain Publishing, March 15, 2004.
- Thinking Strategically, Pocket Mentor,

Harvard Business Review Press. June 17, 2010.

- Simplified Strategic Planning: The No-Nonsense Guide for Busy People Who Want Results Fast, Robert W. Bradford and Brian Tarcy, Chandler House Press, September 2000.
- Strategic Planning for Nonprofit Organizations: A Practical Guide and Workbook, Second Edition, Michael Allison and Jude Kaye, Wiley; 2 edition, July 11, 2003.
- Strategic Planning for Public and Nonprofit Organizations: A Guide to Strengthening and Sustaining Organizational Achievement (Bryson on Strategic Planning), John M. Bryson, Jossey-Bass, July 5, 2011.
- Strategic Thinking: A Step-By-Step Approach to Strategy, Second Edition, Simon Wootten et al, Kogan Page Business Books; 2nd edition, June 2002.
- Learning to Think Strategically (New Frontiers in Learning), Julia Sloan, Butterworth-Heinemann; I edition, June 29, 2006.
- Essential Managers: Strategic Thinking, Andy Bruce and Ken Langdon, DK ADULT; 1st edition, August 1, 2000.

5 Lateral Thinking

LEARNING OUTCOME

- Introduction
- Meaning
- Uses of lateral thinking
- Who Needs Lateral Thinking?
- Need for lateral thinking
- Benefits of lateral thinking
- Techniques of lateral thinking
- How to use lateral thinking
- Lateral thinking exercises
- Books for further reading

> "If you haven't heard of Edward de Bono or of Lateral Thinking, perhaps you have been too busy thinking in conventional ways."
>
> \- Forbes Magazine

Introduction

Edward de Bono coined the term 'lateral thinking' in 1967. It was first mentioned in the book called "The Use of Lateral Thinking" (Jonathan Cape, London)

Lateral thinking is particularly concerned with the generation of new perceptions and new ideas. It involves changing perceptions and flexibility. This may sound the same with creativity since both are concerned with producing something new. But the fact is that lateral thinking is a more precise definition of the process of changing perceptions than creativity.

Lateral thinking is more concerned with the processes where as creativity is concerned with the results. The end product of lateral thinking is insight, not multiplicity of alternatives.

Meaning

Lateral thinking is a way of solving problems by rejecting traditional methods and using unorthodox and illogical means.

Lateral thinking refers to solving problems through an indirect and creative approach. Lateral thinking is about reasoning that is not immediately obvious and about ideas that may not be obtainable by using only traditional step-by-step logic.

Trying to look at the problem from many angles instead of tackling it head-on.

Lateral thinking is a systematic approach to thinking.

Lateral thinking is thinking out of the box by expanding one's horizons.

Uses of lateral thinking

Once a person acquires the lateral thinking attitude he need not need to be told when and where to use lateral thinking.

- Constructively challenge the status quo to enable new ideas to surface
- Find and build on the concept behind an idea to create more ideas
- Solve problems in ways that don't initially come to mind
- Use alternatives to liberate and harness the creative energy of the organization
- Turn problems into opportunities
- Select the best alternate ideas and implement them

> Lateral thinking is concerned not with playing with the existing pieces but with seeking to change those very pieces.
>
> -Edward de Bono

Who Needs Lateral Thinking ?

Lateral thinking can benefit persons mentioned below.

- People who devise strategies,
- people who work in R & D,
- people holding position which require innovation,
- idea generation, concept development,
- creative problem solving,
- fast changing trends,
- fierce competition, and
- fields where strategies are developed to challenge the status quo can benefit from Lateral Thinking

Need for lateral thinking

> The way you think, the way you behave, the way you eat, can influence your life by 30 to 50 years.
>
> Deepak Chopra

With the ever changing and increasing pressure to provide added value in everything that is done and to sustain in the business, it has become a necessity for managers to adopt lateral thinking.

In an increasingly competitive world, traditional methods of doing may not take one so far. People need to go beyond to generate new concepts and new ways of doing things.

1. Competition and trends

Business opportunities involve fierce competition and fast changing trends.

2. Changing business situations

To keep pace with these situations, a disciplined process of innovation, idea formulation, concept development, creative problem solving and the strategy to challenge these concepts is required.

3. Nurturing natural thinking

Lateral thinking provides unconventional techniques which help you nurture your usual thinking to produce enhanced results.

> Traditional thinking is all about "what is", Future thinking is all about what can be.
>
> Edward de Bono

Benefits of lateral thinking

Brings creative thinking into sharp focus:
Creates new ideas to enhance productivity:
Challenges current thinking:
Increases the number of creative ideas:
Innovation in problem solving skills:

> If your thinking is sloppy, your business will be sloppy. If you are disorganized, your business will be disorganized.
>
> -Michael Gerber

Techniques of lateral thinking

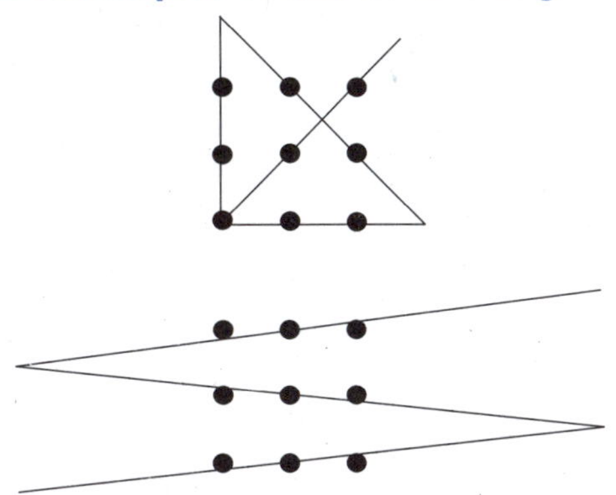

1. Develop alternatives: Produce as many new ideas as possible.

2. Focus: Focus on what has to be achieved in particular.

3. Challenge the existing methods : To get the desired results change your ways of operations. Same operations are expected to produce same results.

4. Selecting the best : Select the best ideas and develop them into possible approaches

5. Domesticate the ideas : Develop ideas and convert them to fit into one's business.

How to use lateral thinking

Lateral thinking can be used in a variety of situations.

- Constantly challenge the status quo methods of operations to get new ideas.
- Try to solve problems in ways that don't initially come to mind
- Use alternatives to develop creative energy in the organization
- Turn problems into opportunities
- Select the best alternate ideas and implement them

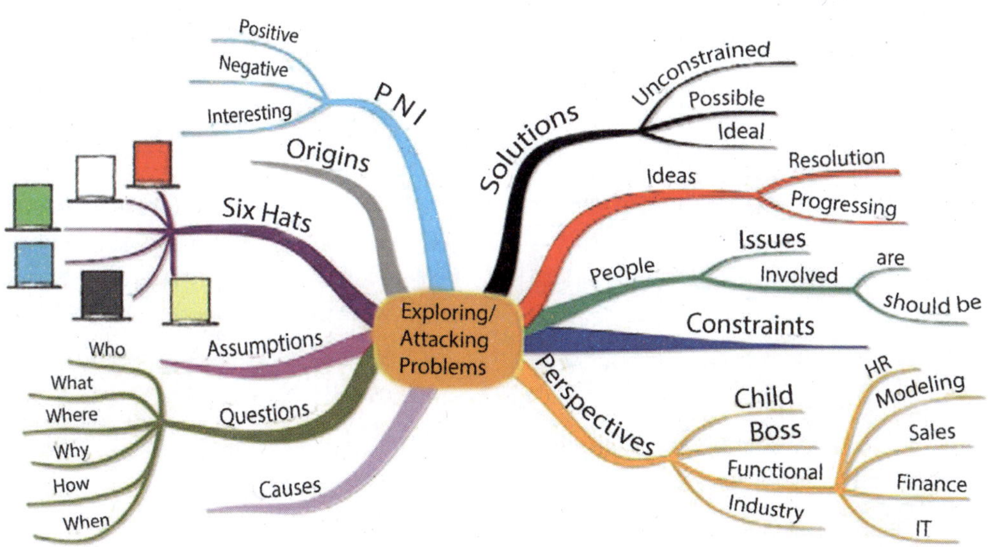

> We should accomplish many more things if we did not think of them as impossible.
>
> – Vince Lombardi

Lateral thinking exercises

1. What can you hold in your right hand, but not in your left?
2. How many animals of each species did Moses take into the Ark?
3. A man built a rectangular house, each side having a southern view. He spotted a bear. What colour was the bear?
4. If you were alone in a deserted house at night, and there was an oil lamp, a candle and firewood and you only have one match, which would you light first?
5. What can you put in a wooden box that would make it lighter? The more of them you put in the lighter it becomes, yet the box stays empty.
6. Which side of a cat contains the most hair?
7. The 60th and 62nd British Prime Ministers of the UK had the same mother and father, but were not brothers. How do you account for this?
8. How many birthdays does a typical woman have?
9. Why can't a man living in Uttarpradesh be buried west of the River Ganges?
10. Divide 40 by half and add ten. What is the answer?
11. To the nearest cubic centimetre, how much soil is there in a 3m x 2m x 2m hole?
12. Is it legal for a man to marry his widow's sister?
13. If you drove a coach leaving Red fort with 35 passengers, dropped off 6 and picked up 2 at Rashtrapathi Bhawan, picked up 9 more at, dropped off 3 at Rajghat, and then drove on to arrive in London 40 minutes later, what would the name of the driver be?
14. A woman lives on the tenth floor of a block of flats. Every morning she takes the lift down to the ground floor and goes to work. In the evening, she gets into the lift, and, if there is someone else in the lift she goes back to her floor directly. Otherwise, she goes to the eighth floor and walks up two flights of stairs to her flat. How do you explain this?
15. A window cleaner is cleaning the windows on the 25th floor of a skyscraper, when he slips and falls. He is not wearing a safety harness and nothing slows his fall, yet he suffered no injuries. Explain.
16. The band of stars across the night sky is called the "...... Way"?
17. Yogurt is made from fermented ....
18. What do cows drink?
19. A farmer has 15 cows, all but 8 die. How many does he have left?
20. If a red house is made of red bricks, and a blue house is made of blue bricks, what is a green house made of?
21. In what sport are the shoes made of metal?
22. If a plane crashes on the Italian/ Swiss border, where do you bury the survivors?
23. If the hour hand of a clock moves 1/60th of a degree every minute, how many degrees will it move in an hour?
24. How many hands does the clock of Big Ben have?

25. How many times do the hands of a clock overlap in 24 hours?
26. John's mother has 3 children, one is named April, one is named May. What is the third one named?
27. You are running in a race. You overtake the second person. What position are you in?
28. In the same race, if you overtake the last person, then you are in what position?
29. A cowboy rode into town on Friday, spent one night there, and left on Friday. How do you account for this?
30. How can you throw a ball as hard as you can, and make it stop and return to you, without hitting anything and with nothing attached to it?
31. A man and his son were in a car crash. The father was killed and the son was taken to hospital with serious injuries. The examining doctor exclaims: "But, this is my son!".

    How can this be?
32. There are 23 football teams playing in a knockout competition. What is the least number of matches they need to play to decide the winner?
33. Sarah's father has five daughters. The oldest is called Lala, the next Lele, the third Lili, the fourth Lolo. What is the fifth daughter's name?
34. You have to choose between three rooms.

    The first is full of raging fires

    The second is full of tigers that haven't eaten in 3 years.

    The third is full of assassins with loaded machine guns.

    Which room should you choose?
35. Name three consecutive days in English without using the words Tuesday, Thursday, or Saturday

Answers:

1. Your left hand, forearm or elbow.
2. None. NOAH built the Ark
3. White. Only at the North Pole can all four walls be facing South.
4. The match!
5. Holes
6. The outside
7. Churchill was Prime Minister twice, from 1940 to 45 and from 1951 to 55.
8. One
9. Because he is still alive .
10. 90. Dividing by half is the same as multiplying by 2.
11. None - it's a hole!
12. No - because he's dead
13. YOU are the driver!
14. The woman is of small stature and couldn't reach the upper lift buttons.
15. He was cleaning the inside of the windows.
16. Milky Way
17. Milk
18. Water. After the previous two questions, did you answer milk?
19. Eight
20. Glass
21. Horse racing
22. You don't bury survivors!
23. One
24. Eight: there are four faces to the clock of Big Ben (see the picture to the right)
25. 22: the minute hand will go round the dial 24 times, but the hour hand will also complete two circuits. 24 minus 2 equals 22.
26. John
27. If you overtake the second person then you become second.

28. You can't overtake the last person in a race!
29. His horse was named Friday.
30. Go outside and throw it upwards.
31. The doctor was his mother. Going full circle, this is very similar to the first question.
32. In a knockout competition, every team except the winner is defeated once and once only, so the number of matches is one less than the number of teams in this case 23-1 = 22.
33. Sarah.
34. The second room. Tigers that haven't eaten in three years are dead!
35. Yesterday, today, and tomorrow.

Out of interest this particular puzzle is where the expression "to think outside the box" originally came from.

> "Great business competitors are great lateral thinkers . . ." - **Edward de Bono**

Exercise

1. How many babies are seen?

2. Who is the murderer?

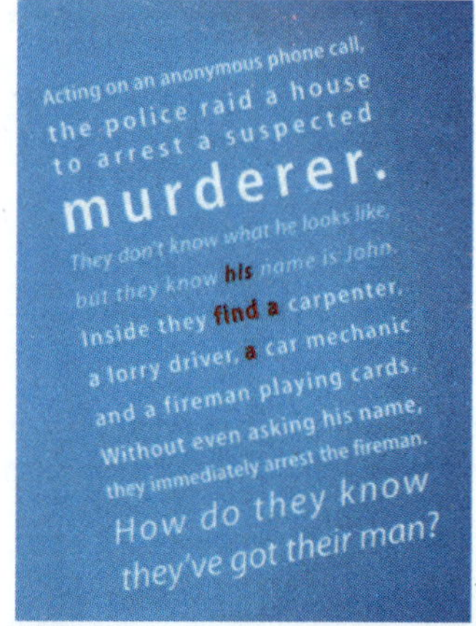

3. Can you solve this puzzle?

Take the second glass from the left, pour its contents into the fifth glass from the left then return it to its original position

Books for further reading

- Lateral Thinking: Creativity Step by Step (Perennial Library, Edward de Bono, Harper Perennial; Reissue edition, 31 July 1990.
- The Leader's Guide to Lateral Thinking

Skills: Unlocking the Creativity and Innovation in You and Your Team, Paul Sloane, Kogan Page; 2nd edition ,November 28, 2006.

- Lateral Thinking: A Textbook of Creativity, Edward de Bono, Penguin, 12 Nov 2009.
- How to Have Creative Ideas: 62 exercises to develop the mind, Edward de Bono, Vermilion, 26 April 2007.
- Outstanding Lateral Thinking Puzzles, Paul Sloane and Des MacHale, Sterling, September 1, 2005.
- Creativity Workout: 62 Exercises to Unlock Your Most Creative Ideas, Edward De Bono, Ulysses Press ,March 1, 2008.
- Six Thinking Hats, Edward De Bono, Back Bay Books; 2 edition, August 18, 1999.
- Hall of Fame Lateral Thinking Puzzles: Albatross Soup and Dozens of Other Classics, Paul Sloane and Des MacHale, Puzzlewright; Reprint edition, May 3, 2011.
- Lateral Thinking Posers: More Than 100 Brainteasers to Solve With Logical Reasoning, Erwin Brecher, Carlton Publishing Group, June 1, 2011.

6 Boss–Subordinate Relationship

LEARNING OUTCOME

- Managing Your Boss
- Steps in building relationship with the boss
- Dealing with difficult boss
- Working for a female boss
- Working with subordinates
- Steps in building relationship with your subordinates
- Key behaviours in managing others
- Books for further reading

Use your head to understand yourself & use your heart to understand others

Managing Your Boss

In any place of work one has to report to a boss, manager or supervisor. It is the workplace reality. One's relationship with his boss affects how he feels about his job and the overall work environment. In fact it is the basis for staying in a job. Motivation to work isn't all about money anymore. It is the relationship in the work place that matters a lot.

The relationship with the boss is important and in fact it is a pointer to subordinates loyalty and commitment to the organization. Subordinates who have positive relationship with their boss are likely to be more committed to the organization than those who do not. Factors that contribute to the type of relationship between boss and subordinates include mutual support, trust, liking, attention, performance, and loyalty.

You are often remembered not for what you spoke but for how you spoke. Dr. K. Alex

Steps in building relationship with the boss

Towards creating a winning relationship the following tips are recommended:

1. Understanding the boss

The subordinates should appreciate the boss's goals, his work pressure, his strength and also understand his weakness. One cannot change the basic personality of the boss but can always avoid misunderstanding by knowing his strength and weaknesses.

2. Understanding yourself

The boss is only one half of the relationship. The other half depends on the subordinates. Developing a good relationship requires that one should know his own strengths, weaknesses and personal style.

3. Developing and managing a relationship

With a clear understanding of one's boss and himself, one can usually establish a way of working together that fits both.

4. Compatible work styles

A good working relationship with a boss depends on the style adopted by the subordinates. Some bosses are readers and some are listeners. To readers the ideas should be presented in a report and to the listeners the ideas are to be explained. Creating a compatible relationship involves drawing on each other's strengths and making up for each other's weaknesses.

5. Mutual expectations

Some superiors spell out their expectations very explicitly but most do not. Ultimately the burden falls on the subordinate to find out what the boss's expectations are. Developing a workable set of mutual expectations also requires the subordinates to communicate their own expectations to the boss.

6. A flow of information

Managing the flow of information upward is very difficult. Nevertheless for the good of the organisation the subordinates are expected to convey the success and well as failures.

7. Dependability and honesty

Dishonestly is another issue. Dishonesty is the most troubling trait a subordinate can have. Without a basic level of trust a boss has on his subordinates the relationship is going to be sour.

8. Good use of time and resources

The boss has limited time and energy. Every the subordinates meet their bosses they make use of or waste those resources. So one should be wise to make use of those resources selectively. Do not waste their time and energy on small issues.

9. Contribute Profitable business Initiatives

Generally business is established for profitability. Generate business related initiatives that will help the boss and team to achieve the Organization's objectives.

10. Be a Solution Bank

Bringing problems to the boss's table at all times will question the subordinate's competence. That will present him as a time waster and have a negative effect on your appraisal. In reality, bosses will appreciate subordinates with good problem solving skills.

> Look at the sun you see time. Look at heart you see love. Look at eyes you see life

Dealing with difficult boss

People may not get ideal bosses to work with. Sometimes they may have to work with tough bosses. Here are some ways of dealing with difficult bosses.

The first step is to make sure that everything one does is right. This will eliminate the chances of the boss pointing fingers at mistakes.

Jot down the behaviour of the boss. His or her likes, dislikes, what irks him/her the most. Analyse these and accordingly stay away from, or pay detailed attention to certain things.

When an employee is being criticised by his boss, he should not get defensive. This will invite more trouble considering that the boss is already bad. Listen to what he/she has to say and discuss the matter later.

Try to be as professional as possible. Make sure to treat the work seriously and give him/her little reason to complain.

Document all the work. Every note of appreciation of the work; should be preserved to vouch for the reliability and proof of one's hard work.

If the boss is found a difficult personality, matter can be referred to the HR department. They might be able to sort it out in an amicable way.

Lastly, if the boss is found just unbearable it's best to leave the company.

All good things start from the heart and all bad things start from the mind.

Working for a female boss

Working for a female boss is not so much different from working for a male boss. It is not something to be cautious of. In fact it can be an enjoyable experience. Here are some tips to work for a female boss.

1. Learn her likes and dislikes.

Identify her likes and dislikes with dereference to the work situations. Find out if needs a typed report or a mail. Find out if she needs to be informed personally or over the phone.

2. Be proactive.

The subordinates need to be proactive. They should not wait for their bosses to come to their table. Subordinates should ensure that they are in her room with the report when they are expected.

3. Convince her.

Convince her of your ability as an individual as well as a team player. Help her in creating a friendly atmosphere.

4. Appreciate her work.

Tell the boss that you appreciate her supervisory and managerial skills. Everyone likes to be complemented and female are not exception to it.

5. Be trust worthy.

The subordinates have to prove their female bosses that they are trust worthy and reliable. Trusting the bosses always helps to build a relationship.

> I suppose leadership at one time meant muscles; but today it means getting along with people.
>
> – Mahatma Gandhi

Working with subordinates

With the complexity of today's workplace, subordinates have a role to play in leading within an organization; hence, leading up and down is essential to create a winning strategy.

Some bosses/managers are strong in technical side but may be weak in interpersonal relationships. They find the going tough in building relationship with their subordinates. To develop a healthy and cordial relationship one needs to get acquaintance with his subordinates, learn their names, their work, their strengths and weaknesses and their attitude. Here are some steps to build a better relationship with your subordinates.

Steps in building relationship with your subordinates

Relationship by Job Title

The relationship with one's subordinate depends on the job title one holds. The power vested with the boss/manager decides the kind of perception his subordinates hold on them. Without the power the boss/manager is like a peer working with them.

Relationship by Job Knowledge

The boss/manager's knowledge in the job boosts his authority over his subordinates. When the subordinates come with questions, problems and challenges the boss/manager should be able to come with answers and solutions.

Relationship by Respect

Apart from the knowledge and skills the boss/manager has, what matters is the attitude that he exhibits. This is one of the major ingredients to maintain the positive relationship with the team. If the boss can coach his subordinates with enthusiastic attitude, he can always win the respect from his team under your leadership. The boss/manager should respect the subordinates as he is respected.

> Man becomes great exactly in the degree in which he works for the welfare of his fellow-men.
>
> Mahatma Gandhi

Key behaviours in managing others

- Respond instead of React
- Show appreciation
- Remember peoples' names accurately
- Giving importance to their feelings
- Drop criticism
- Speak positively of others
- Encourage
- Remind people of what they do well
- Manage expectations

Books for further reading

- Career Dynamics: Managing the superior/ subordinate relationship, Lloyd Baird, Kathy Kram, Spring Publication, 1983.
- Improving employer-employee relationships: a biblical and Talmudic perspective on human resource management, Gordon Cohn, et al, MCB UP Ltd, 2002.
- Handbook of Organizational Behavioir, Alderfer, C. A, NJ: Prentice-Hall, 1986.
- Interpersonal competence and organizational effectiveness, Argyris, C., London: Tavistock Publications, 1962.
- The workplace within, Hirschhorn, L, Cambridge. MA: MIT Press, 1988.
- Managers can drive their subordinates mad, Kets de Vries, Manfred, Harvard Business Review July-August, 1979.
- Internal a world and external reality: Object relations theory applied, Kernberg, O, New York: Jason Aronson, 1980.
- The Worth of the Individual, the Value of Work, and the Power of the Mind, Joseph T. Allmon, Xlibris Corporation, 2010.
- My job, my boss, and me: gaining control of your life, David Lee Woods, Lifetime Learning Publications, 1980.
- Improving the Boss - Subordinate Relationship, Patrick A. Notaro, Northern Illinois University, 1971.
- Modern Human Relations at Work, Richard M. Hodgetts, Kathryn W. Hegar , Cengage Learning.,2011
- Good Boss, Bad Boss: How to Be the Best... and Learn from the Worst, Robert I. Sutton, Business Plus, 07-Sep-2010.
- You Can't Fire Everyone: And Other Lessons from an Accidental Manager, Hank Gilman, Penguin Group USA, 17-Mar-2011
- How to Become a Great Boss: The Rules for Getting and Keeping the Best Employees, Jeffrey J. Fox, Hyperion, 15-May-2002.

7 Facing Changes

LEARNING OUTCOME

- Adapting change
- Understanding change
- Examples of Organizational Change
- Truth about change
- Dealing with Change Misconceptions
- What Happens when an Organisation Undergoes Change?
- Changes Related to People
- Changes Related to Organizations
- Changes Related to Systems
- Change management
- Responsibility for managing change
- Involve not impose
- Principles of change management
- Change and Business Development
- Five basic principles of change management
- Why people resist change:
- Change Management Model
- Why change management fails (Kotter)
- Introducing change
- Dealing with defensive employees
- Books for further reading

> Only the wisest and stupidest of men never change. Confucius

Every organisation has to change with time, failing which, it stands the risk of becoming obsolete in the field. Change must be carried out at the regular and needed intervals. Change could be brought in the policy, procedure, infrastructure, staff, and as required. Whatever is the change introduced, there is going to be resistance. This should not prevent a boss /manager introducing changes. One should develop a leadership force that will face the combined force of resistance.

Adapting change

Adapting change is crucial for an organization. Organizations inevitably encounter changing conditions that they are powerless to control. Adaptation might involve establishing a structured methodology for responding to changes in the business environment or establishing coping mechanisms for responding to changes in the workplace.

Terry Paulson, the author of *Paulson on Change, quotes*: "It's easiest to ride a horse in the direction it is going." In other words, don't struggle against change; learn to use it to your advantage.

> One key to successful leadership is continuous personal change.
> – Robert E. Quinn

Understanding change

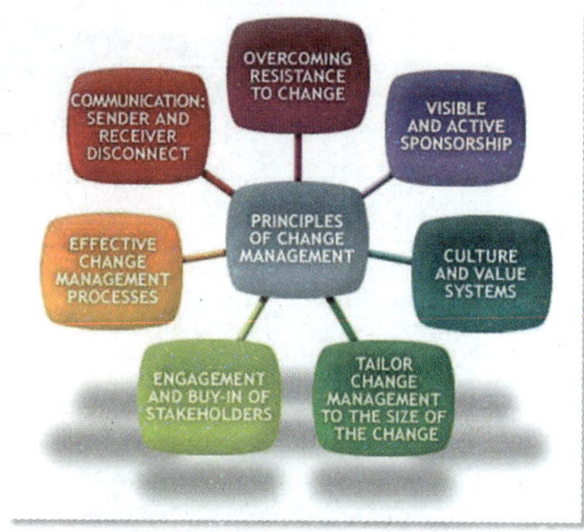

Change may appear to be about changing jobs, places, products, etc. But it occurs first inside people's heads. When organizations try to change without understanding this invisible element, any change is understood to a problem and failure.

> Personal change is a reflection of our inner growth and empowerment.
> Robert E. Quinn

Examples of Organizational Change

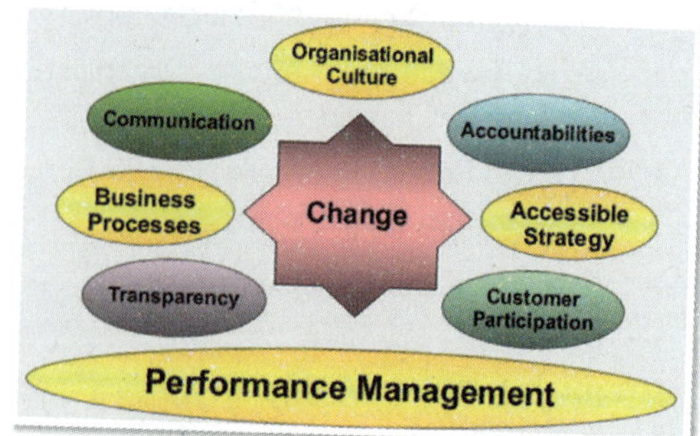

1. Missionary changes
2. Strategic changes
3. Operational changes (including Structural changes)
4. Technological changes
5. Changing the attitudes and behaviors of personnel

> Whosoever desires constant success must change his conduct with the times.
> Niccolo Machiavelli

Truth about change

- Emotional reactions are at least as important as any other aspect of implementing change.
- The higher the involvement in change, the less negative the inevitable reactions.
- The intensity of emotional reaction is proportionate to the speed of change.
- The unresolved effects of change are cumulative.
- Rewards and incentives can cause people to change, but they will not neutralise their feelings of loss.

> Every generation needs a new revolution. Thomas Jefferson

Dealing With Change Misconceptions

- Change happens quickly
- Survivors are glad they have a job
- Time takes care of everything
- Everyone who is not on board has something wrong with them
- The weak people are the ones who leave
- People "hear" what senior management communicates
- People take senior management communication at face value
- If the communication is done "right" the first time, it is enough
- By changing the formal relationship, how we "do business" will change
- Pressures that caused the change will be seen in a rational manner.
- These misconceptions require a thoughtful approach from those leading change.

> Your success is based on your ability to change faster than your competitor, customers and business.
> Mark Sanborn

What Happens when an Organisation Undergoes Change?

People feel anxiety when there are

major changes within their organisation. They are often uncertain of their future, and the future of their colleagues in the organisation. Consequently the following fear of change reactions may occur.

CHANGE MANAGEMENT

Missing - opportunities, job, status, security taken away

Alone - nobody understands, the unlucky one

Lethargic- commitment goes, energy levels drop

Limits - each person has limits to the amount of change they're comfortable with

Enough - when those limits are reached they cry enough and resist further change

Revert - people easily revert back to known behaviours

Some of the common reactions to change result in the following behaviours at work:

Drop in morale

Drop in work outputs and

Drop in productivity

Drop in Manager's credibility

Drop in Commitment to the organisation and work

Drop in levels of service

> Change is like death and taxes that cannot be avoided. Dr.K.Alex

Changes Related to People

Culture Change

Culture change in an organization aims at changing the behaviour patterns of the employees. reward-and-recognition programs, employee empowerment, and training are some of the examples of cultural changes.

People-centered Change

This type of change attempts to alter the attitudes, behaviors, skills, or performance of employees in an organization. Communication, employee motivation, leadership, and group interaction are some examples of people-centered change.

Social Change

Social change encompasses the large set of goals that organizations establish around people. Empowered workforce, collaborative work arrangements, and matching personal fulfilment to organizational needs are some of the examples.

Changes Related to Organizations

Leadership Change: Many significant changes – in policy, people, organizational structure, procedures are introduced simultaneously with a leadership change.

Structural Change : Structural changes may involve structural characteristics, administrative procedures, or management systems.

Reengineering: This focuses on making major structural change in the organization and focuses on everyday tasks or procedures. The aim is to improve productivity, efficiency, quality, or customer satisfaction.

Fundamental Organizational Change: Fundamental organizational change focuses on changing major characteristics of the entire organization rather than specific parts.

Acquisition: Acquisition is the process through which one company takes over the controlling interest of another company.

Merger

Merger is the combining of two or more entities into one. Merger differs from a consolidation..

Consolidation

Consolidation is the combining of separate companies, functional areas, or product lines, into a single organization.

Strategic Change

Strategic changes involve long-term planning and incorporating a strong external orientation. These changes may cover major functional areas of an organization. This type of change may occur when adjusting the firm's strategy to achieve the goals of the company.

Changes Related to Systems

Process-oriented Change

Process-oriented change refers to changes in the way in which an organization delivers services, produces products, or handles current business practices.

Technological Change

This refers to the implementation or integration of technology into the processes of an organization.

Systems Change

Systems change refers to changes at the heart of the organization. It means impacting change across all elements of the system.

Benchmarking

"Benchmarking is the search for best practices. Benchmarking allows your organization to see what others are doing, what is working for them and what to avoid.

> The most successful businessman is the man who holds onto the old just as long as it is good, and grabs the new just as soon as it is better.
>
> Robert P. Vanderpoel

Change management

Change management is a structured approach to shifting individuals, teams, and organizations from a current state to a desired state. It is an organizational process aimed at empowering employees to accept and embrace changes in their current business environment.

> To improve is to change, to be perfect is to change often.
>
> Winston Churchill

Change management has three different aspects. They are adapting to change, controlling change, and effecting change. A proactive approach to dealing with change is at the core of all three aspects. For an organization, change management means defining and implementing procedures to deal with changes in the business environment and to profit from changing opportunities.

Successful change management is more likely to occur if the following are included:

1. Benefits management and realization to define measurable stakeholder aims, create a business case for their achievement
2. Effective Communications that informs various stakeholders of the reasons for the change, the benefits and the details of the change
3. Devise an effective education, training and skills to understand change
4. Provide personal counselling to alleviate any change related fears.
5. Monitoring of the implementation and fine-tuning as required.

NAME	WHAT WAS HE/SHE?	WHAT DID HE BECOME?
Albert Einstein	Ordinary Patent Clerk	World Famous Scientist
Abraham Lincoln	Poor Farmer's Son	President Of America
Goldameir	Average School Teacher	Prime Minister Of Israel
Franklin. D Roosevelt	Sick And Both Legs Paralysed	President Of America
Homer	Blind	Greatest Greek Writer
Helen Keller	Blind, Deaf And Dumb	Renowned Writer
Demosthenes	Nervous Stammerer	Well Known Greek Orator
Beethoven	Deaf	Renowned Music Composer
Thomas Edison	Matriculate	Greatest Inventor
M.S. Oberoi	Simple Clerk	One Of The Biggest Chain Hotel Owner In The World
K.K. Patel	Son Of An Ordinary Farmer	Largets Seller Of Nirma Washing Powder (₹ 1200 Crores Turnover)
Topiwala	Fresh Matriculate With Initial Investment Of ₹ 100/-	Now Sells ₹ 5 Crore Worth Shingar Bindi Per Year
Malathi Holla	Polio Striken (25 Surgeries Done)	Got 150 Gold Medals In Disc Throw, Etc.
Shard Kumar Deekshit	2 Heart Attacks; Crippled In Lower Side Of The Body; Vocal Cords Removed	Performed 45,000 Surgeries Free Of Cost
C.N. Janaki	Both Legs Polio	Famous Swimmer, Name In Book 'Special People' By Oxford University

Responsibility for managing change

The employee does not have a responsibility to manage change. Responsibility for managing change is with management. They must manage the change in a way that the employees can cope with it. The manager has a responsibility to facilitate and enable change. The manager's role is to interpret, communicate and enable employees to understand change.

Involve not impose

Whenever an organization imposes new things on people there will be difficulties. Participation, involvement and open communication are the important factors while introducing change. Workshop and seminars are very useful processes to develop collective understanding, approaches, policies, methods, systems, ideas, etc.

Change cannot be imposed on people. People need to be educated to find their own solutions with support from managers, and tolerance and compassion from the leaders and executives. Leadership style is more important than clever process and policy.

Principles of change management

1. Involve and agree support from people within system
2. Understand where the organisation is at the moment
3. Understand where one wants to be

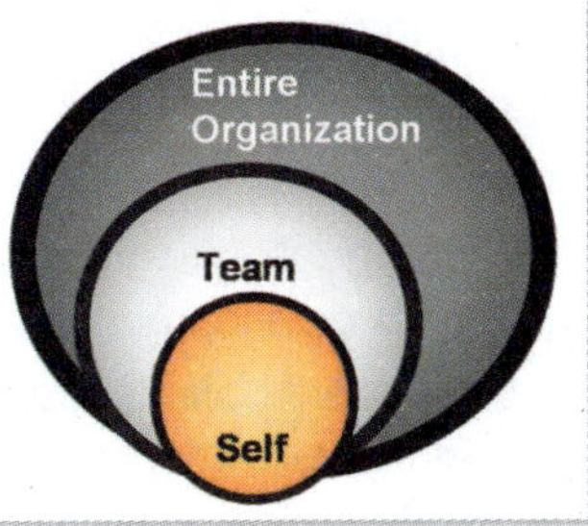

4. Understand when, why, and what measures will be taken to be there
5. Communicate, involve, enable and facilitate involvement from people, as early and openly and as fully as is possible.

> When I was an young man, I wanted to change the world. I found it was difficult to change the world, when I found I couldn't change the nation I began to focus on my town. I couldn't change the town and as an older man, I tried to change my family. Now, as an elderly person I realise the only thing I can change is myself. And suddenly I realise that if, long ago, I had changed myself, I could have made an impact on my family, My family and I could have changed the town. An impact on our town, their impact could have changed the nation.
>
> An unknown monk 1100 A.D

Change and Business Development

There are so many ways to develop a business which achieve growth and improvement. Change can be introduced in the following fields.

- sales development
- new product development
- new market development
- business organization, shape, structure and processes development
- tools, equipment, plant, logistics and supply-chain development
- people, management and communications development
- strategic partnerships and distribution routes development
- international development
- acquisitions and disposals

Five basic principles of change management

Change management is a basic skill in which most leaders and managers need to be competent. There are very few working environments where change management is not important. When leaders or managers are planning to manage change, there are five key principles that need to be kept in mind:

1. Different people react differently to change
2. Everyone has fundamental needs that have to be met
3. Change often involves a loss, and people go through the "loss curve"
4. Expectations need to be managed realistically
5. Fears have to be dealt with

Why people resist change:

1. Lack of communication

People may only understand the change in broad terms and not in practical terms. They may not see what they should do differently.

2. Procedure

People may resist change because the staff may not know how it should go about it. They may lack the knowledge, skills and experience to implement the proposed change.

3. Goal oriented

Another reason why the people may resist change is that they do not know why they should undertake a specific change. They may not be convinced about the purpose of the change or they may not see the benefits of the change.

4. Involvement of parties

Resistance may also arise if people are not clear about who are specifically involved in the change. Too many parties involved in the change without a clear definition of their roles will bring confusion.

> People don't resist change. They resist being changed. Peter Senge

5. Proper support

Commitment to change from the top is critical. Many well-planned change programmes have failed because leaders who plan the change do not follow up with the necessary support. Support in terms of resources, know how, moral support and motivation is needed to ensure smooth implementation of change.

6. Lack of courage

Change programmes often fail because of absence of courage to implement the change. Managers do not create a safe environment for people to experiment or try new things. People feel that it is risky to undertake any change.

7. Poor motivation

There are many change programmes that failed due to lack of motivation rather than the lack of know-how. A clear declaration on how people are going to be rewarded if they achieve successful results from change would benefit the people a lot.

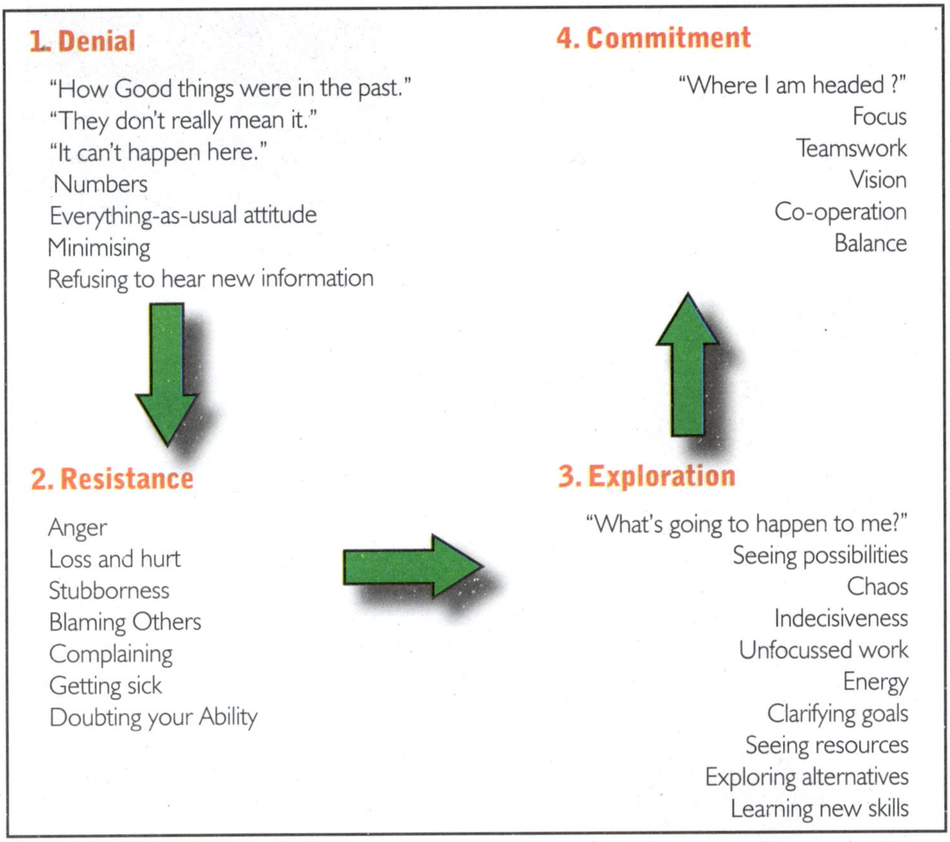

1. Denial

"How Good things were in the past."
"They don't really mean it."
"It can't happen here."
Numbers
Everything-as-usual attitude
Minimising
Refusing to hear new information

2. Resistance

Anger
Loss and hurt
Stubborness
Blaming Others
Complaining
Getting sick
Doubting your Ability

3. Exploration

"What's going to happen to me?"
Seeing possibilities
Chaos
Indecisiveness
Unfocussed work
Energy
Clarifying goals
Seeing resources
Exploring alternatives
Learning new skills

4. Commitment

"Where I am headed ?"
Focus
Teamswork
Vision
Co-operation
Balance

Change Management Model

Dealing With Change

1. Denial

The first response to a significant change is often shock, - a general refusal to recognise the information. In this way people protect ourselves from being overwhelmed. Common responses include:

- Denying: "This can't be happening."
- Ignoring: "Wait till it blows over."
- Minimising: "It just needs a few minor adjustments."

2. Resistance

Resistance is about fear of change. People may become physically ill, feel all sorts of physical, emotional, or mental symptoms. Some people may doubt their ability to survive the change. During this phase there is a greater focus on mourning the past, more than preparing for the future.

3. Exploration

After a period of struggle, individuals and organisations usually emerge from their negativity, breathe a sigh of relief, and shift into a more positive, hopeful, future-focused phase.

4. Commitment

Finally, the individual has broken through the problems, discovered new ways of doing things or adapted to the new situation. The commitment phase begins with focus on a new course of action.

> I'll go anywhere as long as it's forward. David Livingstone

Why change management fails (Kotter)

In his book "Force for Change Kotter" lists the following as the main reasons why change fails:

- Allowing to much complexity
- Failing to build a substantial coalition
- Understanding the need for a clear vision
- Failing to clearly communicate the vision
- Permitting roadblocks against the vision
- Not planning and getting short-term wins
- Declaring victory too soon
- Not anchoring changes in corporate culture

> Our only security is our ability to change . John Lilly.

Introducing change

The growth and survival of organizations depend upon change and the way in which those changes are introduced. When a change takes place it is perceived as a threat to employees socially, psychologically, or economically.

The important aspect in gaining employee acceptance is the relationship that exists between the supervisor introducing the change and the employees who are affected by it. How the supervisor introduces the change has more to do with resistance than the change itself.

Reducing Resistance to Change

1. Supply appropriate information.

Explain as early as possible what will happen, why, and how employees and the department will be affected.

2. Encourage employee participation.

Allow employees to share in making decisions about it.

> The world hates change, yet it is the only thing that has brought progress.
>
> – Charles Kettering

Dealing with defensive employees

1. Attacking a person who is being defensive only makes that person more defensive.
2. People become defensive when they feel they are being attacked.
3. Sometimes a manager needs to back off when an employee is being defensive and try again another time.
4. The best defense against defensiveness is to be open and honest, to communicate clearly, and to listen responsively.

Books for further reading

- Leading Change, John P. Kotter, Harvard Business Review Press, August 7, 1996.
- The Dance of Change: The Challenges to Sustaining Momentum in Learning Organizations, Peter M. Senge et al, Crown Business, March 16, 1999.
- Change the Way You Lead Change: Leadership Strategies that REALLY Work, David Herold and Donald Fedor, Stanford Business Books, June 6, 2008.
- The Six Secrets of Change: What the Best Leaders Do to Help Their Organizations Survive and Thrive, Michael Fullan, Jossey-Bass, November 29, 2011.
- Change Leader: Learning to Do What Matters Most, Michael Fullan and Jossey-Bass, July 26, 2011.
- Leading in a Culture of Change, Michael Fullan and Jossey-Bass, June 20, 2001.
- Life Changes: A Guide to the Seven Stages of Personal Growth, Spencer and John D. Adams ,Paraview press, 2002.
- Facing Changes, Ron Clark, Presbyterian Christian Education, 1984.
- When you are Facing change, Andrew D. Lester, Westminster/John Knox Press, 1989.
- Facing Changes, Changing Faces: Positive Spiritual and Emotional Growth in Mid-Life, Alvin Marcetti, Shirley Lunn, Darton, Longman & Todd, Limited, 1995.
- Self Development for Managers: Managing Change, Colin Carnall, Routledge, 1991.
- Managing change, Christopher Mabey, Bill Mayon-White – 1993.
- Managing Change, Bernard Burnes, Pearson Education, Limited, 10-Dec-2009.
- Managing the Dynamics of Change: The Fastest Path to Creating an Engaged and Productive Workforce, Jerald M. Jellison, McGraw-Hill Professional, 06-Jun-2006.
- Deep change: discovering the leader within, Robert E. Quinn, Jossey-Bass Publishers, 31-Jul-1996.
- Building the Bridge As You Walk On It: A Guide for Leading Change, Robert E. Quinn, John Wiley & Sons, 12-Apr-2004.
- Epic Change: How to Lead Change in the Global Age, Timothy R. Clark, John Wiley & Sons, 21-Dec-2007.
- Resistance to Change: A Guide to Harnessing Its Positive Power, Thomas R. Harvey, Elizabeth A. Broyles, Rowman & Littlefield Education, 30-May-2010 .
- Courage to Change: A Paradigm for Success, Shirley Summer, SummerTime Press, 01-Feb-1993.

Facing Challenges

LEARNING OUTCOME

- Introduction
- Panicky people
- Negative people
- Positive people
- What does facing challenges / taking initiative mean?
- Why is it important for youth to face challenges and take initiative?
- Benefits of Facing challenges
- Things to consider when setbacks occur:
- Facing challenges in life
- Books for further reading

Introduction

"God allows testing in our lives for good ... not to punish us, but to PURIFY us."

Have you ever noticed that every challenge also contains a blessing in disguise? If not, you may not have been looking closely enough! It's true that challenges often seem like inconveniences when they get in the way of something you want. When you're working toward goals that are important to you, the last thing you want is to face a big challenge or obstacle because it usually means that your desired outcome will be delayed.

However, if you learn to see challenges in a new light, they can easily become the best things that have ever happened to you.

The secret to a happy and peaceful life is to understand that your personal challenges are in your life for a reason - to help you grow. If you choose not to grow from them you will remain stuck in their consequences and are doomed to repeat the same challenges again and again.

Relish your challenges. Thank God for them. Learn from them. Grow because of them and move on to the next ones with positive anticipation and gratitude.

Life is not easy, hard, challenging, fun, or rewarding. Life just is, what it is. "Why do some people have it easier with more money, better relationships, successful careers, a lot of playtime and travel? Why do some struggle to pay their bills and balance all of the requirements as a mother or father, business owner or employee? The answer lies in the way one faces the challenges in life.

The test of courage comes when we are in the minority. The test of tolerance comes when we are in the majority. Ralph W. Sockman

Life is a series of challenges, whether large or small. How one handles his challenges depend on how one responds his day today challenges -does he panic and become frantic or does he stay positive and energetic, does he make big problems small and small problems big. All these normal events will determine how he is going to face those bigger challenges.

Panicky people

Panicky people don't have control over their mental energies. Their minds are unfocused, and so they exaggerate events. Their confusion complicates things and even small challenges appear to be big problems. They generally react emotionally to situations, so they easily become irritable, anxious, and excitable. These qualities make them undependable.

> Worry does not empty tomorrow of its sorrow; it empties today of its strength. Corrie Ten Boom

Negative people

Negative people make everything a problem. They undergo a great amount of mental and physical stress. When they face with challenges they say things like, "It's too difficult. I can't do it. I never did it before. I don't know how. Why is this happening to me?"

Positive people

Positive people never buckle under pressure , or hesitate to do what needs to be done. They treat every challenge as a wakeup call. They keep telling that if we are resourceful, challenges are easy to overcome. They take initiative to fix solutions to problems.

- Sir Edmund Hillary was unsuccessful on three different occasions in his attempt to climb Mt. Everest before his successful summit in 1953. People who lauded the praises of his triumphant ascent said, "You've conquered the mountain," and Sir Hillary said, "No, I've conquered myself." The bitter experiences of the three failed attempts did not hold back Hillary from a fourth one. With strong will, and relentless enthusiasm, he pursued his goal and achieved it.

> Nobody will believe in you unless you believe in yourself.
>
> – Liberace

What does facing challenges / taking initiative mean?

Some young people choose to participate in diverse and challenging activities, remain motivated in the face of obstacles, and persist until they accomplish their goals. These youth are said to have initiative. Initiative is the motivation to direct effort toward achieving challenging goals and remain determined even when things get difficult (Larson, 2000).

> It is not because things are difficult that we do not dare; it is because we do not dare that they are difficult.
>
> – Seneca

Developing this initiative requires three key things: intrinsic motivation; deliberate, goal-directed action in real-world situations and sustaining goal-directed efforts over time (Larson, 2000). What this means is that young people with initiative

- Are personally invested in their activities;
- Exert attention, effort, and concentration in complex and challenging real-world situations; and
- Continue working to achieve their goals, even if it involves re-evaluating and adjusting their strategies in the face of setbacks (Larson, 2000).

Why is it important for youth to face challenges and take initiative?

The ability to face challenges and take initiative is also important for young people because it is essential to becoming a life-long learner. Life-long learners, who must be equipped to direct their own learning and

development (especially following their formal schooling), are characterized as demonstrating perseverance, initiative, and adaptive abilities

However, even before young people get into the world of work, they must be able to take initiative to meet challenges on their own. In middle school, and certainly in high school and college, students face more challenging homework, are required to initiate their own studying, and are held responsible for completing a wide range of assignments Clearly, as they move on to enter a challenging workforce in this "information age" where the need for technical knowledge and skills is ever-growing, young people will have to be self-initiated learners to succeed.

Finally, young people who can face challenges and take initiative are more able to avoid participation in a number of problem behaviours.

> Perseverance is not a long race; it is many short races one after another.
>
> – Walter Elliott

> What lies behind us and what lies before us are tiny matters compared to what lies within us.
>
> – William Morrow

- Create projects, programs, and organizations that (1) are youth-based and motivate young people to determine the direction and goals of the activities, (2) engage young people in environments that include real-world challenges that are well-matched to their abilities, and (3) involve activities that are continued over time and require young people to monitor, regulate, and plan for the course ahead.
- Encourage young people to evaluate their performances according to objective criteria rather than the judgments of others.
- Avoid constructing program environments based on an extrinsic reward system; instead, provide benchmarks that all young people can use to measure their progress and accomplishments, regardless of their varying abilities and levels of experience;
- Provide concrete, process-oriented feedback instead of simply saying "good job" or "try harder";
- Give young people choices about what and activities to engage in how to accomplish their projects
- Help young people generate new strategies when they do not achieve what they intend to achieve
- Teach young people how to set specific, challenging short-term goals, rather than vague long-term goals

Benefits of Facing challenges

> To succeed you must first improve, to improve you must first practice, to practice you must first learn.
>
> – Wesley Woo

Generally speaking, there are only really two ways to address difficulties:

1. You can either change the circumstances surrounding the difficulty, or;
2. Change yourself to better deal with the circumstances or the difficulty itself.

You can deal with difficulties properly and leverage your experience (or better yet the experience of others) to enhance your confidence, or you can deal with them incorrectly and let them seriously damage your confidence, performance and ultimately your reputation.

1. What Can I Learn From This?

Too often we view challenges as annoyances or personal vendettas, when in fact they may hold a great opportunity to learn and grow! If you start by asking what you can learn from each challenge, you'll suddenly see them as possibilities that pave the way to greater wisdom and self-mastery.

2. How Can This Strengthen Me?

One major reason why challenges intimidate us is because we don't feel capable of handling them. We have a limited perception of our own abilities, so we automatically believe that the challenge is bigger than we are. However, if you learn to see challenges as an opportunity to become stronger and more empowered, there's no way they can hold you back!

3. How Can I Use This to My Advantage?

Most often we see challenges as disadvantages – but is that necessarily true? A challenge can often help you see that there are many possible ways to achieve a goal, and the one you've chosen may not necessarily be the best one. Asking this question can often open your mind to alternative routes that may be shorter or otherwise better in some way.

4. How Can I Use This to Help Others?

Though we often believe our goals affect only ourselves, more often we have a huge impact on the people around us too. Not only do other people watch what you do and how you live your life – they often model their own behaviour after yours! If you refuse to let challenges intimidate you or slow you down, you just might inspire and motivate others to do the same with their own challenges.

5. What Would Make This a Worthwhile Experience?

Sometimes just being willing to recognize that a challenge may not be such a bad thing can be enough to help you realize all kinds of wonderful benefits from it. This question does a couple of things: first, it helps you feel more empowered because it affirms that you have a choice in how you react to the challenge; and secondly it reminds you that every challenge holds the seeds for unlimited blessings and opportunities.

> Challenges will always create opportunities, but you can only find them when you start to see challenges as opportunities.

Things to consider when setbacks occur:

Just as a diamond cannot be polished without friction, neither can you fully develop your skills without them being tested by adversity. Use obstacles and failures as an opportunity to polish your skills. I think Winston Churchill said it best when he noted, "The pessimist sees the difficulty in every opportunity; the optimist sees the opportunity in every difficulty."

> Life is difficult for those people who expect it to be easy. Scott Peck

1. Be honest enough to acknowledge what has happened. Don't hide from the reality of the situation at hand. Setbacks happen... don't be discouraged, learn from them, deal with them, and move on.

2. Turn setbacks into development opportunities by asking positive questions such as: What are the positives surrounding this situation? How can I make the most of this situation? What can I learn from it? What are the facts underlying this problem? How can I avoid this situation next time?

3. Acknowledge the fact that setbacks occur to everyone and you are not being singled out.

4. View setbacks as a challenge to overcome rather than an issue or problem.

> The ultimate measure of a man is not where he stands in moments of comfort and convenience, but where he stands at times of challenge..."
>
> Dr. Martin Luther King, Jr

Facing challenges in life

Life will always have challenges:

Just get used that mindset.Life is always full of challeneges for every person whatever section of society he belongs to.If a poor person wants to get out of his poverty to a comfortable living standard he has to struggle it out.Same goes for a middle class person if he wants to get a more comfortable life...he too has to struggle it out.So challenges will always exist.

More challengers you encounter more successful you become:

Life always has various levels of games for every individual. For a person overcoming one challenge, he become mentally ready for other one in course of which life gives him greater rewards for solving those challenges.You go to another level by stretching your comfort zone a little further.

Every challenge gets an opportunity:

Every challenge a person acquires in life presents him with two kinds of opportunities... one is personal growth and other one financial growth.So it's a real challenge to spot these opportunities and to cash on them thus leading to personal and material development of one self.

Recognise opportunity:

The best way to recognize an opportunity in adversity is to get guidance and learn from the same people who have been through your path.They are your best teachers.Since every one cannot be accessible at a given time,reading books,listening to audio tapes from personal development experts can go a long way in helping you.

Put your learnings into action:

The important part of learning in life is to put whatever one has learnt into action. Without action all the strategies of life have no meaning.So if you want to profit in you life mentally as well as finanacially start from today to put into action whatever good things learnt from life before your time runs out!!

Books for further reading

- How to Overcome Great Challenges, Barbara Mills, Author House, 13-May-2011.
- Be the Hero: Three Powerful Ways to Overcome Challenges in Work and Life, Noah Blumenthal, Marshall Goldsmith, Berrett-Koehler Publishers, 01-Aug-2009.
- Never Give Up! Relentless Determination to Overcome Life's Challenges, Joyce Meyer, FaithWords, 17-Mar-2009.
- Overcoming the Challenges of Life, Ifeanyi Enoch Onuoha, Author House, 2011.
- Self Power: Spiritual Solutions to Life's Greatest Challenges, Deepak Chopra, Ebury Publishing, 05-Apr-2012.
- Switch: How to Change Things When Change Is Hard, Dan Heath and Chip Heath, Random House of Canada, 2010.
- Even a Small Star Shines in the Darkness: Overcoming Challenges Faced by .., Tretip Kamolsir,Proquest,2008
- Everyday Heroes Overcome Challenges, Jill C. Wheeler, Abdo & Daughters Pub., 01-Sep-1996
- Great Consulting Challenges and How to Surmount Them: Powerful Techniques for the Successful Practitioner, Alan Weiss, Jossey-Bass/Pfeiffer, 2003.
- Dealing With and Overcoming the Challenges of the 21st Century: You Have What It Takes, Just Keep the Focus and a Positive Attitude, Cecily Mwaniki, Author House, 2010.
- Courage to Overcome: Finding Faith to Face Your Challenges and Win!, Marcus C. Taylor, Brownstone Publications, LLC, 2010.

9 Staying Motivated

LEARNING OUTCOME

- Defining motivation
- Staying motivated at work place
- Staying motivated in negative work environment
- Keeping the workers motivated during crisis.
- What are the reasons for lack of motivation and enthusiasm?
- Staying Motivated When You Work From Home
- Books for further reading

> Motivation is a fire from within. If someone else tries to light that fire under you, chances are it will burn very briefly. Stephen R. Covey

There is a common problem that people face both at the work place and at home- the problem of staying motivated. People develop interest for new things initially but as the years pass by they lose their motivation in doing those same work or learning something new. They start giving excuses like losing focus, being discouraged, boring, having too much to do, not free to learn and so on. But what bothers is that they are not achieving as much as they are capable of.

The solution is staying motivated. The fact is that people do the things they are intensely motivated to do. Ask any teenager how hard they'll work to get the assignment ready. Ask a college student how many sleepless night he spent to pass an important term paper in the college. When people are motivated, nothing can stand in their way!

> I never did anything by accident, nor did any of my inventions come by accident; they came by work..
> – Thomas A. Edison

Defining motivation

Now the question is what is motivation and how to stay motivated? Motivation is simply that which gives purpose and direction to behaviour. Motivation is what drives you to behave in a certain way or to take a particular action. Motivation is the driving force by which people achieve their goals. It is the incentives that people seek.

Staying motivated

It happens for people that at times their work becomes so difficult that it starts affecting their performance and self-motivation and pep talk don't work. And if this is not corrected at the right time often a good worker's efforts go down the drain and the person is labelled as another average employee.

How to remain Motivated? One must be clear of his/her goal or dream. One should be able to achieve anything and everything if he is able to define them. The goal must be specific, measurable, attainable, and time bound.

Start every day by reviewing and re-affirming your most important objectives. Every day, one has to read, listen and speak to exciting people and surround oneself with things that energize. This world is full of negative energy and plenty of negative people. To counter this, one has to surround himself with things that energise, challenge and excite.

It is not a secret that the key to achieve one goal after the other is to stay motivated. There may be tasks that one may not like, still if one understand and recognizes the need and their importance he is likely to stay motivated. Here are some ways to stay motivated.

> Work as though you would live forever, and live as though you would die today.
>
> – Og Mandino

Staying motivated at work place

1. Ensure goal clarity

Working without having a clear vision, mission, and objectives will demotivate the people. People will be wasting their time and energy without a clear vision and they will end up doing unimportant things. People should clarify that there are no uncertain vision and mission while performing a task. It is always noticed that with clear vision and mission the goals are attained comfortably.

2. Develop clear strategy

Having clarified one's vision and mission, one has to formulate strategies to achieve the same. Split big projects into small manageable tasks which generally are interesting as compared to the big projects. Developing a blueprint of the tasks split will provide meanings to one's daily routine. The more organized one is the more motivated one will be and less likely to panic.

3. Try to succeed in whatever you do

Success in itself is a big motivator. Work hard to achieve the desired results and you will experience inner motivation to success further. With the clearly defined goals and strategies, the secret of success will be hard work. Try to ride the wave of each success to further the next success.

4. Reward yourself

Develop the practice of rewarding yourself as and when you achieve your desired goals. Plan in advance what forms of reward and what project will be rewarded. This will give you something that extra drive to get there and a sense of excitement and enthusiasm when you attain your desired goals.

5. Remind yourself of the objectivity of life

It is important to keep things in perspective and always remind yourself of the purpose of life and why you work. Apart from money, it is about realizing your potential, feeling alive and useful, making a difference in the world, expressing creativity, expanding your skills and abilities, helping others and contributing to the community. Also remember that work is work and that you have a life outside of work to look forward to, enjoy and make a difference in.

> To finish first, you must first finish.
>
> – Rick Mears

6. Maintain a healthy work/life balance

Maintaining a healthy work/life balance is essential both for your general motivation level and your overall wellbeing. Make sure you take the time to do the things you like to do outside of work be it connecting with friends and family, exercising, reading, taking courses, shopping or other hobbies and activities that channel your creativity and energy. Having something to do after work will see you through moments of difficulties at work when your motivation and energy levels are not as high as they could be.

7. Stay positive

Staying positive endures your energy and staying negative drains it. Staying positive increased your speed and staying negative does the other way around. Avoid negative feelings and concentrate on the positive. To do this, you have to listen to motivational tapes, to music, read motivational books, talk to inspired or inspiring people, surround yourself with positive stimuli and concentrate on the reasons you work. Count your blessings at every opportunity.

8. Take different approach

learn to do things in a different way to stay motivated in work. you may perform the tasks effectively, still a different approach will do the trick of staying positive. changing the approach generally opens up new possibilities.

9. Watch your progress

watching the progress would not just mean tracking it but recognizing it. Recognizing is taking time to look at a bigger picture and realize where exactly you are, and how much more you have left to do.

> The man who does not work for the love of work but only for money is not likely to make money nor find much fun in life.
>
> – Charles Schwab

Staying motivated in negative work environment

You may not be blessed with an ideal environment to work. There may be difficult situations to deal with to stay motivated. The situations may be quiet unwilling and hostile. The company you work for may be experiencing a big slump and may be people around you are asked to leave week after week. If your job is like this, it is difficult to get out of bed and go to work in the morning.

It is even more difficult to go to work with a smile on your face and keep it on for the entire day. And, it becomes increasingly difficult to want to continue to put in the extra effort when not only are you not getting recognized for it, but you are getting reprimanded for not getting more done or recognized for the great job done.

How is anyone supposed to work in an environment like this? And people might ask, why would anyone want to stay there? there may be hundred and one reasons starting from family, health, children education, transportation, to proximity to the office, but what is most important is how to cope with these situations without pulling out your hair.

Here are some ways to stay motivated in a negative work environment.

1. Focus on the positive

It is absolutely difficult to stay motivated in a negative work environment, but dwelling on the problem is not going to resolve any of your problems. All the more negativity breeds more negativity. Focusing on positive can be just as contagious as negative feelings.

If you can manage to maintain a positive outlook despite the darkness surrounding you, it will help you in your work environment.

2.Leave work at the job

When you work in a unfriendly work environment it is hard to check those problems at the door of the work place when you leave for the day. For many, the problems stay with them even after going home for the day. The best practice is to check those problems and prevent them from entering your home. if you are bringing them home it means you are not leaving the office, and the agony continues at home. it is difficult to get motivated if you don't take a break from your issues and problems.

3. Take breaks at regular intervals.

Whenever you are chained to your desk, do not forget to take breaks. Many forgo or forget to take breaks. These breaks often will help you to stay motivated. These breaks are often seen as a disturbance but in reality it helps you to recharge your batteries.

4. Work more and smarter.

With the financial crisis throughout the world, many companies go for lay-offs, cutting the budgeted figures, and reducing allowances it is wise to change your life style accordingly. To continue to get the benefits you were getting before, you need to work more and smarter.

5. Encourage your coworkers.

Encourage your coworkers without deploying your power or authority. This will help the coworkers to stay motivated and it helps to stick together.

> If you want to gather honey, don't kick over the beehive. Dale Carnegie

Keeping the workers motivated during crisis.

Traditional methods fail to motivate an employee when the crisis deepen. Bonuses, extra vacation days, contests, and awards may no longer work. during the crisis the employees lose their sense of security, stress level goes up, and lose their concentration in their work.

So what can companies do to keep employees motivated at work during crisis? Here are important courses of action. In case you are an employee you can pass on this writing to your boss.

1. keep them informed

During crisis employees are frightened by the state of uncertainty and they need to be informed as much as possible about what is going on in the company. They should never be kept in the darkness. When they are not informed or less informed they are likely to imagine the crisis bigger and deeper than what it actually is. Have meetings at regular intervals and keep sending letter.

2. Reassure and prepare

Communicate to your employees the steps taken to make their jobs secure. Inform them of the other measures taken if they have to leave their current position and take up a new assignment. Keep them also informed of the worst of situations and support the company is prepared to offer. Convene workshops to face changes that may be in the offer.

3. Listen.

Bring in an outsider/couneller/facilitator to help employees vent their fears. Many employees feel that this is one of the most helpful tools to keep employee motivation high. The employees also feel that the fear shared is fear reduced and it also helps them to come out of loneliness.

4. Celebrate.

Having followed the first three steps, it is advisable to hold a get together. A few hours of relaxed moments during crisis, relives the tension. It is also a chance for the management to convey the feelings that the company is with them and cares for them.

> Work and play are words used to describe the same thing under differing conditions. Mark Twain

What are the reasons for lack of motivation and enthusiasm?

- Absence of enough stimuli or incentive
- Being too stressed or nervous.
- Fear of failure, due to failure in the past.
- Fear of what others might say.
- Lack of enough interest.
- Lack of faith in one's abilities.
- Laziness.
- Low self-esteem.
- No awareness of the importance and usefulness of the subject or goal.
- Not having the time to delve into the subject or goal.
- The feeling or belief that there are other more important things to do.
- The habit of procrastination.

> My father always told me, "Find a job you love and you will never have to work a day in your life." Jim Fox

Staying Motivated When You Work From Home

A good way to establish an effective work routine at home is to identify how you work. you can be motivated to work by internal forces. you don't need a supervisor with a stopwatch and a notice board to get you on task. you are naturally disciplined to achieve your targets.

Here are some tips to work from home.

1. Create a Work-friendly Space

Make your work place filled with light and energy. put up calendars and surround yourself with visual reminders. Ensure that you have everything you need at your fingertips and make sure that your communication devices are reliable and efficient, to make the task of staying in touch with the outside world.

2. Get a Mentor

If you feel that you are down with motivation, take the help of a mentor. ensure that you meet the mentor in a stimulating environment. ensure a formal mentoring relationship to make you more comfortable and look for ways in which your mentor can expand your network.

> It is better to wear out than to rust out.
> – Richard Cumberland

3. Establish a Routine

Set up a plan and schedule and use automatic reminders and weekly calls to keep you on track. Identify the areas of your routine that are the hardest to stick to and establish strategies to mitigate.

4. Communicate your Needs

Talk with family and friends about your needs and expectations to help you stay on track. Communication not only helps you to improve the way you work, but gives those around you a new insight into another facet of your life.

Books for further reading

- Motivation That Works: How to Get Motivated and Stay Motivated, Zev Saftlas, Coaching With Results, January 14, 2004.
- 100 Ways to Motivate Yourself: Change Your Life Forever, Steve Chandler and Career Press, July 31, 1996.
- Motion before Motivation: The Success Secret That Never Fails, Michael J. Dolpies, Ocean View Publishing, LLC, June 1, 2010.
- Drive: The Surprising Truth about What Motivates Us, Daniel H. Pink, Riverhead Hardcover; 1 edition, December 29, 2009.
- Your Best Life Now: 7 Steps to Living at Your Full Potential, Joel Osteen, Faith Words; 1st Trade edition, August 20, 2007.
- The Little Book of Coaching: Motivating People to Be Winners, Kenneth H. Blanchard, Don Shula, Harper Collins Business, 29-May-2002
- Motivation: Theory and Research, Harold F. O'Neil, Michael Drillings, Routledge, 1994.
- Great Motivation Secrets of Great Leaders, John Baldoni, Mcgrawhill, 2004.
- Human Motivation, David C. McClelland, Cambridge University Press, 1984.
- Motivation and personality, Abraham Harold Maslow, Robert Frager, Harper and Row, 1987.
- Think and Grow Rich: Complete Original, Unaltered Text: Special 70th .., Napoleon Hill, Arc Manor LLC, 2007.
- Understanding motivation and emotion, Johnmarshall Reeve, Wiley, 2005

Effective Decision Making

LEARNING OUTCOME

- Decision Making Process
- Methods of Decision Making
- Steps in DM
- Theoretical Approaches to Incividual Decision Making
- Optimizing Decision Theory
- The Subjective Expected Utility Model
- Steps to Effective Decision-Making
- Effective Decision Making in Teams
- Methods for team decision making
- Confusion and decision making
- Decision making styles
- Books for further reading

> Stay committed to your decisions, but stay flexible in your approach.
> – Tony Robbins

You make a lot of decisions every day. From the clothes that you wear, the food you will eat, and the attitudes you will have for the day. Some decisions are more difficult and some of them are so easy. Effective decision making is an art. If you master it, you will be able to go through life's challenges more smoothly.

You can make more effective decisions when you know what the key elements and the factors are. Your decisions should be action-oriented. If you can't act on your decisions, then it's a waste of time. You should also be able to respond to feedback once you implement your decision. What looks good on paper may not work when you actually test it.

> The hardest thing to learn in life is which bridge to cross and which to burn.
> – David Russell

Decision Making Process

According to Peter Drucker there are 5 elements of an effective decision making process:

1. Problem rationalization. The clear rationalization that the problem was generic and could only be solved through a decision that establishes a rule or a principle. Know the problem you are solving.

2. Boundary conditions. The definition of the specifications that the answer to the problem has to satisfy, that is, of the "boundary conditions." Know your range of options that will still count as success.

3. The Right Thing to Do. Before you decide what's feasible, first figure out what the right thing to do is.

4. Action. Turn decisions into action.

5. Feedback. Get feedback on what's working and what's not.

Methods of Decision Making

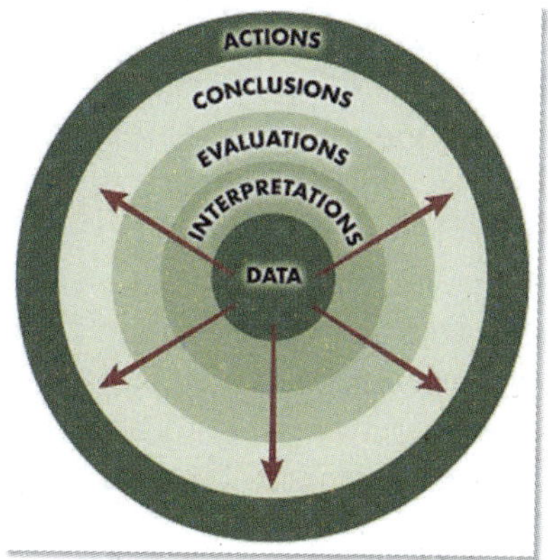

According to Patterson, Grenny, McMillan, and Switzler, there are four common ways of making decisions:

1.Command

This is a method where decision are made with no involvement at all. The subordinates are only conveyed on what was decided by the bosses. This takes place under two circumstances. Namely where there is an external forces are involved or the bosses wanted their decisions to be implemented.

2.Consult

This is a method whereby others are invited to give their suggestions before the bosses make their choice. Consultations are done with experts, representatives, and parties concerned. consulting is a way of gaining ideas and support. you should gather ideas, evaluate options, make a choice and then inform the people concerned.

3.Vote

Voting is suitable to situations where efficiency is the highest value and particularly when you're selecting from a number of good options. When facing several decent options, voting is said to be best method because it saves lot of time, but should never be used when team members don't agree to support whatever decision is made. In these cases, consensus is required.

4.Consensus

Consensus means that you talk until everyone honestly agrees to one decision. This method is said to be both a great blessing and a frustrating curse. it is said to be a blessing because everyone honestly accepts the decision taken and curse because it takes lot of time and energy. This method can produce tremendous unity and high-quality decisions. If misapplied, it can also be a horrible waste of time.

> The doors we open and close each day decide the lives we live.
>
> Flora Whittemore

Steps in DM

A significant part of decision making skills is in knowing and practicing good decision making techniques. One of the most practical decision making techniques can be summarized in those simple decision making steps:

1. **Identify the purpose of your decision.** What is exactly the problem to be solved? Why it should be solved?

2. **Gather information.** What factors does the problem involve?

3. **Identify the principles to judge the alternatives.** What standards and judgement criteria should the solution meet?

4. **Brainstorm and list different possible choices.** Generate ideas for possible solutions.

5. **Evaluate each choice in terms of its consequences.** Use your standards and judgement criteria to determine the cons and pros of each alternative.

6. **Determine the best alternative.** This is much easier after you go through the above preparation steps.

7. **Put the decision into action.** Transform your decision into specific plan of action steps. Execute your plan.

8. **Evaluate the outcome of your decision and action steps.** What lessons can be learnt? This is an important step for further development of your decision making skills and judgement.

Theoretical Approaches To Individual Decision Making

Optimizing Decision Theory

Based on decisions made by individuals, the scientists have developed some theories in decision making. The "optimizing" type of theory. Optimizing theories make a number of assumptions about how people make decisions. First, decision makers are believed to consider all possible decision options. Second, decision makers are seen as assessing all of the available information when making their choice. Third, decision makers are seen as choosing that option that provides them with the best possible outcome.

The Subjective Expected Utility Model

It is an equation that allows individuals to predict the decision that individual people will make when faced with a number of options. Use of this model implies that people act as if they had calculated the "expected utility" of each option. When people do this, they choose the alternative that they believe has the highest expected utility.

> Good decisions come from experience, and experience comes from bad decisions.
>
> – Author Unknown

Steps to Effective Decision-Making

Here are tens tips to effective decision-making that could guide you in making the right choice.

1. Define your goals and objectives. You can only arrive at a major decision if you know what you want. Otherwise, you will change from one decision to another because you have no idea as to what you are trying to accomplish.

2. Define the problem clearly. Identify what bothers you and if you are not sure do some additional thinking and investigation. There are several related factors to your problem but these should not distract you from understanding what the real problem is.

3. Stay away from anxiety. When people keep shouting at you to decide and circumstances press you to come to a decision and when things are going from bad to worse, stop for a moment and take a long breath. After all you cannot take an effective decision if you are anxious. Try to remove anxiety from your mind and take a fresh look at the problem before you arrive at a decision.

4. Look at the problem from different perspectives. Try to approach the problems from as many angles as possible, like from the angles of the boss, the customers, the society and so on. Put yourself in the shoes of others and understand how they would solve the situation.

5. Ask for advice of others. Look for help whenever in confusion. Involve people like your friends, colleagues, seniors and bosses. remember the fact that you are not alone in this world.

> In any moment of decision the best thing you can do is the right thing, the next best thing is the wrong thing, and the worst thing you can do is nothing.
>
> – Theodore Roosevelt

6. Write down your options. It is always better to write down your actions to understand in its entirety. It is also possible to explore all other options and their implications when the plans are put in black and white.

7. Examine the Implication of the alternatives. Analysing the implications of each alternatives is an important part of your decision making process. Of course it may take lot of your time but you are left with no option. You have to weigh the costs and the benefits of each decision. Deciding things in haste will work against you. So you better make sure that your decision is worth it.

8. Choose the best alternative. After carefully going through the list of your alternatives, choose the best course of action. There will always be limitations in your decision. You may face challenges while implementing your decisions but you will have to stand by it as long as it is good for the organisation.

9. Monitor progress. After making the decision and deciding to do your choice of action, you should monitor your progress. This will help you make adjustments along the way. Depending on your goals, you can make adjustments and additional decisions along the way.

> It's in your moments of decision that your destiny is shaped.
> – Anthony Robbins

Effective Decision Making in Teams

Making decisions is a fundamental life skill, and you have to learn to become better at it. Many a time you work in a group and you may have to take a collective decision. Individual decision making is the act of making up one's mind. Team decision making is the process through which a team chooses an alternative.

Team performance depends largely on the choices made by the team. These choices, in turn, depend on the processes through which teams decide. Therefore, high performance teams require processes through which teams make high quality decisions.

Managers will have to help teams improve their performance and reduce the likelihood of dysfunctional teams by working with subordinates/colleagues to help them improve their capabilities to make team decisions.

> A wise man makes his own decisions, an ignorant man follows the public opinion.
> – Chinese Proverb

Each team has to make many decisions during its existence. These decisions may be made in ad hoc ways or using processes that increase the likelihood of an effective choice. The processes through which decisions are reached may dramatically affect the quality of the decisions and team performance. For example, the choice a design approach might be made by flipping a coin or by thoughtful analysis of the pros and cons of each alternative. To make proper decisions, teams need to learn how others have thought about decision making processes.

> It does not take much strength to do things, but it requires great strength to decide on what to do.
> – Elbert Hubbard

Decision making in groups will be examined from three perspectives.

- **Environments for Decision Making.** The environment that a team creates for discussion plays a critical role in quality of its decisions.
- **Methods for Decision Making.** Teams can arrive at decisions in many different ways. The methods deployed to make decisions are important as the decision itself.
- **Tools for Decision Making.** tools here is referred the design, the strategies, and the documents in support of the decision to be taken.

Skill with environments, methods, and tools for decision making will help you a lot, because you are likely to work with as many teams as possible in your career.

Methods for team decision making

Many types of decision making models can be studied and used by teams. Understanding decision making models allows teams to make desired choices about which model might be most appropriate for the various decisions that they have to arrive at.

Individuals benefit from understanding decision models by becoming aware of how biases can affect on making a decision. Being aware of your biases can help you to overcome one's limitations.

> Life is the sum of all your choices.
> – Albert Camus

As a team, understanding decision-making models is compulsory so that the team can make the best decision is valuable. A decision is described as the best decision on the following conditions. That

1. it would not have been thought of by an individual alone,
2. it is a sound solution to the problem,
3. it is a decision based upon input, as unbiased as possible, from each team member, and
4. addresses the team's goal for the decision-making process.

Johnson and Johnson describe seven methods/processes that a team might use to make a decision.

Decision made by authority without group discussion

Process: The designated leader makes all decisions without consulting group members.

Strengths	Weaknesses
• Takes minimal time to make decision	• No group interaction
• Commonly used in organizations	• Team may not understand decision or be unable to implement decision
• High on assertiveness scale	• Low on cooperation scale

Suitability

- Simple, routine, administrative decisions; little time available to make decision; team commitment required to implement the decision is low.

Decision by expert

Process: Select the expert from group, let the expert consider the issues, and let the expert make decisions.

Strengths	Weaknesses
• Useful when one person on the team has the overwhelming expertise	• Unclear how to determine who the expert is
	• No group interaction
	• May become popularity issue or power issue

Suitability

- Result is highly dependent on specific expertise, clear choice for expert, team commitment required to implement decision is low.

Decision by averaging individuals' opinions

Process: Separately ask each team member his/her opinion and average the results.

Strengths	Weaknesses
• Extreme opinions cancelled out	• No group interaction, team members are not truly involved in the decision
• Error typically cancelled out	• Opinions of least and most knowledgeable members may cancel
• Group members consulted	• Commitment to decision may not be strong
• Useful when it is difficult to get the team together to talk	• Unresolved conflict may exist or escalate
• Urgent decisions can be made	• May damage future team effectiveness

Suitability

- Time available for decision is limited; team participation is required, but lengthy interaction is undesirable; team commitment required to implement the decision is low.

Decision made by authority after group discussion

Process: The team creates ideas and has discussions, but the designated leader makes the final decision. The designated leader calls a meeting, presents the issue, listens to discussion from the team, and announces her/his decision.

Strengths	Weaknesses
Team used more than methods 1–3	Team is not part of decision
Listening to the team increases the accuracy of the decision	Team may compete for the leader's attention
	Team members may tell leader "what he/she wants to hear"
	Still may not have commitment from the team to the decision

Suitability

- Available time allows team interaction but not agreement; clear consensus on authority; team commitment required to implement decision is moderately low.

Decision by minority

Process: A minority of the team, two or more members who constitute less than 50% of the team, make the team's decision

Strengths	Weaknesses
• Method often used by executive committees	• Can be railroading

• Method can be used by temporary committees	• May not have full team commitment to decision
• Useful for large number of decisions and limited time	• May create an air of competition among team members
• Some team perspective and discussion	• Still may not have commitment from team to decision

Suitability

- Limited time prevents convening entire team; clear choice of minority group; team commitment required to implement the decision is moderately low.

Decision by majority vote

Process: This is the most commonly used method in the United States (not synonymous with best method). Discuss the decision until 51% or more of the team members make the decision.

Strengths	Weaknesses
• Useful when there is insufficient time to make decision by consensus	• Taken for granted as the natural, or only, way for teams to make a decision
• Useful when the complete team-member commitment is unnecessary for implementing a decision	• Team is viewed as the "winners and the losers"; reduces the quality of decision
	• Minority opinion not discussed and may not be valued
	• May have unresolved and unaddressed conflict
	• Full group interaction is not obtained

Suitability

- Time constraints require decision; group consensus supporting voting process; team commitment required to implement decision is moderately high.

Decision by consensus

Process: Collective decision arrived at through an effective and fair communication process (all team members spoke and listened, and all were valued).

Strengths	Weaknesses
• Most effective method of team decision making	• Takes more time than methods 1–6
• All team members express their thoughts and feelings	• Takes psychological energy and high degree of team-member skill
• Team members "feel understood"	
• Active listening used	

Suitability

- Time available allows a consensus to be reached; the team is sufficiently skilled to reach a consensus; the team commitment required to implement the decision is high.

Confusion and Decision Making

When you set yourself a big new goal in an area you're unfamiliar with, you're going to go through an initial phase of complete and utter confusion. There's nothing wrong with this. In fact, you should be delighted. It means you're doing things right. But it's not always comfortable. Which is why you need to remember the following 6 Rules of Confusion.

> Nothing is more difficult, and more precious, than to be able to decide.
>
> – Napoleon Bonaparte

1. Put up with temporary disorganisation.

If you want to know whether you're in a state of confused goal-building, there's one way to tell: take a look at your desk. It'll be an absolute mess. The confusion of this stage is always reflected in the confusion of your work space. Because you're trying out different ideas and gathering lots of information, you'll have odds and ends of notes, scraps of paper with ideas on, half-started plans, bullet lists of things to do. Don't worry. This is totally normal. Just make sure you have a clear out frequently and don't lose some of the great seedling ideas hidden in there.

2. Learn to live with frustration.

Along with confusion, the early stage of goal-building is also accompanied with frustration. Well, why are you surprised? If you want something and don't see a quick and easy way to get it, you're bound to feel frustrated. That's OK. It's just your inner child – who always got what it wanted when it wanted it – having a tantrum. The grown-up version has to be a little more restrained. Like Thomas Edison who calmly, patiently and without frustration, carried out over 1000 failed experiments before he discovered the right way to build a light bulb.

3. Grow roots.

I know you may not believe me, but the state of confusion is the most important stage of goal-building. This is the stage that determines whether you're going to succeed or not. You may not believe that. In fact, you may long for a bit of clear daylight where everything is routine, not chaos, orderly not muddled, and plain sailing instead of hitting your head against endless brick walls. But, listen. Think of yourself as a plant that's just been sown. How magnificent a specimen you're going to be isn't determined by above-ground growth, but by below-ground roots.

> Clarity gives strength and Confusion causes weakness
>
> – Dr.K.Alex

4. Keep asking.

"What's The Lesson Here?". Many people who go through the early stages of goal-building measure their progress by how much they're advancing towards their goal. Don't do that. After all, if you're putting down roots, you're probably advancing in all directions except the ones you'll be finally moving in. Instead, measure your progress by what you're learning. When you can learn from every day's confusion and frustration, you're making huge leaps forward. Not just in your knowledge and skills, but in your personal strength. That's why writer Trevor Bentley describes the stage of confusion as "the height of wisdom".

5. Keep your morale high.

If this all sounds too easy, take heart. Having been through many states of confusion and frustration on the route to my goals, I know exactly how it feels. Some days it feels like treading treacle. The rest of the world seems to be getting on with their lives while you're stuck in no man's land. All you want to do is give up and settle for something easier. Well, that's OK... for a brief spell. But don't give up. If you feel down – and it's almost certain you will from time to time – give your morale a boost. Slow down. Chill out. Find some successes. And know with absolute certainty that one day soon you'll come out of the state of confusion and be within reach of your goal.

6. Let the creative process work.

Getting through confusion is inevitable if you stick with it. Why? Because your creative brain will work it out for you. Imagine that your brain is an exact replica of the mess on your desk. Lots of bits of information all unconnected. While your desk won't do anything about it, your brain will. It will try to find connections between all the dead ends. That's why sooner or later, and often in an unguarded moment when you're not expecting it, things will suddenly fall into place. That's when you'll get a eureka moment, an "ah-ah" insight, and a shaft of clear light that means you're coming out of confusion.

Someone once said that trying to reach a big big goal – like making a million pounds (dollars, rupees...) – was no different from learning how to drive a car or play a musical instrument. It's about learning to do something you couldn't do before. The goal may be different in each case but the process is the same. 99 out of 100 people who start the process give up when confusion clouds their way. Why not be the 1 who doesn't?

> If you put off everything "till you're sure of it, you'll get nothing done.
> Norman Vincent Peale

Decision Making Styles

Tell-manager

makes the decision entirely and simply relays it to others

Sell-manager

makes the decision but explains the context, reasons and benefit

Test-manager

selects a preferred course of action, but seeks reaction before

Consult-manager

sets out the problem and possible solutions-manger retains the right

Join-manager

sets out the problem and joins in the discussion-manager has the final say

Participate-manager

participates in a team discussion with no more authority-the team's decision emerges

Books for further reading

- Decisions, Decisions: The Art of Effective Decision Making, David A. Welch, Prometheus Books; 1st edition, January 2001.
- Decision Making and Problem Solving Strategies: Learn Key Problem Solving Strategies; Sharpen Your Creative Thinking Skills; Make Effective Decisions, John Adairs, Kogan Page Publication, February 28, 2010.
- Winning Decisions: Getting It Right the First Time, J. Edward Russo and Paul J.H. Schoemaker, Crown Business; December 26, 2001.
- Effective decision making, Helga Drummond, Kogan Page, 27-Jul-1996.
- Judgment in Managerial Decision Making, Max H. Bazerman, Don A. Moore, John Wiley & Sons, 01-Aug-2008.
- Decision traps: ten barriers to brilliant decision-making and how to overcome them, J. Edward Russo, Paul J. H. Schoemaker, Simon & Schuster, 1990.

- The Go Point: When It's Time to Decide--Knowing What to Do and When to Do It, Michael Useem, Crown Publishing Group, 24-Mar-2009.
- A Primer on Decision Making: How Decisions Happen, James G. March, Chip Heath, Simon and Schuster, 23-May-1994.
- Judgment and Decision Making: An Interdisciplinary Reader, Terry Connolly, Cambridge University Press, 2000.
- Sources of Power: How People Make Decisions, Gary A. Klein, MIT Press, 26-Feb-1999.
- How We Decide, Jonah Lehrer, Houghton Mifflin Harcourt, 09-Feb-2009.
- Harvard Business Review on Making Smart Decisions (Harvard Business Review Paperback Series), Harvard Business Review, Harvard Business Review Press, Pril 12, 2011.

Conflict Resolution

LEARNING OUTCOME

- Meaning of conflict
- Points to be understood before studying conflict resolution
- Features of Conflict
- Sources of conflict
- Common reactions to Conflict:
- Functional aspects of conflict
- Dysfunctional aspects of conflict
- Conflict Management Vs Conflict Resolution
- Meaning of conflict resolution
- Ways of addressing conflict
- Managing conflict
- How to handle the silent treatment
- How to handle the gossips
- How to handle the non-stop talkers
- How to handle interruptions
- How to handle abuse or threatening behaviour
- When a situation has progressed to crisis stage
- How to handle high emotions
- How to handle anger
- Healthy and unhealthy ways of managing and resolving conflict
- Steps for conflict resolution
- Steps for on-line conflict resolution:

> People who fight fire with fire usually end up with ashes.
> – Abigail VanBuren

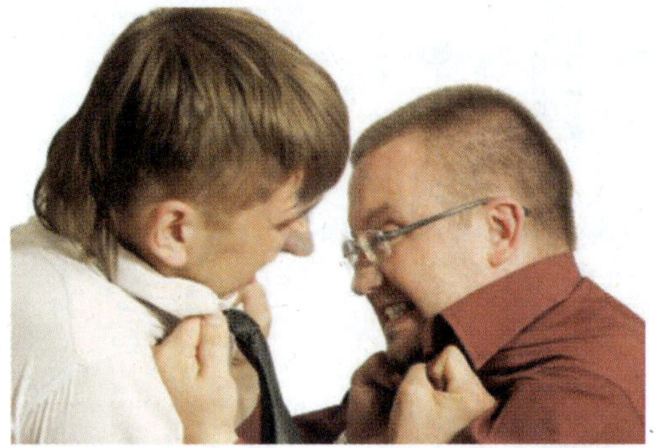

There cannot be a world without conflict and in fact it is not possible to have one such world. As a matter of fact conflict is a normal and necessary part of healthy relationships. After all, two people can't be expected to agree on everything at all times, particularly at the work place.

In many cases, conflict in the workplace just seems to be a fact of life. There are situations where different people with different goals and needs have come into conflict. The fact that conflict exists, is not necessarily a bad thing: As long as it is resolved effectively, it can lead to personal and professional growth.

In many cases, effective conflict resolution has brought in many positive outcomes. However, if conflict is not handled effectively, the results can be damaging. Conflicting goals can quickly turn into personal dislike. Teamwork breaks down. Talent is wasted as people develop dislike for their work.

If you're to keep your team or organization working effectively, you need to solve the conflicts as and when they arise. Therefore, learning how to deal with conflict rather than avoiding it is crucial and also essential.

> Don't let your Yesterday to spoil your Today
> Dr. K. Alex

Meaning of conflict

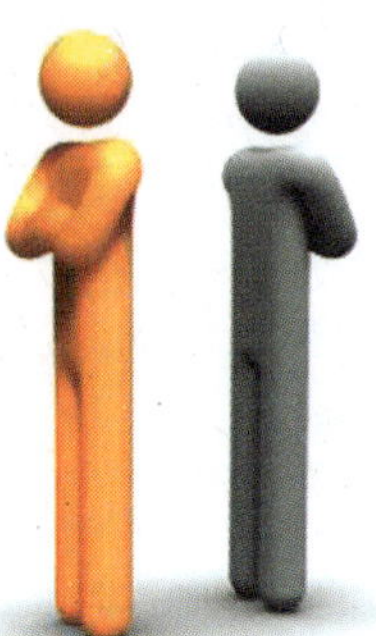

Conflict is a mental and/or physical disagreement in which people's values or needs are in opposition to each other.

> Whenever you see darkness, there is extraordinary opportunity for the light to burn brighter. – Bono

Points to be understood before studying conflict resolution

1.A conflict is more than a mere disagreement

It is a situation in which people perceive a threat (physical, emotional, power, status, etc.) to their well-being. As such, it is a meaningful experience in people's lives, not to be shrugged off by a mere, "it will pass…"

> There are two ways of meeting difficulties: You alter the difficulties or you alter yourself meeting them.
> – Phyllis Bottome

2.Perceptions play a bigger role than the reality.

As such, people filter their perceptions (and reactions) through their values, culture, beliefs, information, experience, gender, and other variables. Conflict responses are both filled with ideas and feelings that can be very strong and powerful guides to our sense of possible solutions.

3. Involvement of substantive, procedural, and psychological dimensions

In order to best understand the threat perceived by those engaged in a conflict, we need to consider all of these dimensions.

4. Conflicts are normal experiences within the work environment.

They are also, to a large degree, predictable and expectable situations that naturally arise as we go about managing complex and stressful projects in which we are significantly invested. As such, if we develop procedures for identifying conflicts likely to arise, as well as systems through which we can constructively manage conflicts, we may be able to discover new opportunities to transform conflict into a productive learning experience.

5. Creative problem-solving strategies are essential to conflict management.

We need to transform the situation from one in which it is 'my way or the highway' into one in which we entertain new possibilities that have been otherwise elusive.

> A pessimist sees difficulty in every opportunity; an optimist sees opportunity in every difficulty.
> – Winston Churchill

Features of Conflict

- **A conflict is more than just a disagreement.** It is a situation in which one or both parties perceive a threat which may or may not be real.
- **Conflicts continue to fester when ignored.** conflicts continue to grow if ignored ,because conflicts involve perceived threats to the relationship, well-being and survival. They stay with us until you face and resolve them.
- **We respond to conflicts based on our perceptions** of the situation, not necessarily to an objective review of the facts. Our perceptions are influenced by our life experiences, culture, values, and beliefs.
- **Conflicts trigger strong emotions.** Conflicts generally trigger strong emotions. They generally make you to feel uncomfortable.
- **Conflicts are an opportunity for growth.** When you're able to resolve conflict in a relationship, it builds trust. You can feel secure and know that your relationship can survive challenges and disagreements.

> Every word has three definitions and three interpretations.
> – Costa Rican proverb

Sources of Conflict

> Many promising reconciliations have broken down because, while both parties come prepared to forgive, neither party comes prepared to be forgiven.
> – Charles Williams

There are many reasons for conflict in any work setting. Some of the primary reasons are:

- **Poor Communication:** Different communication styles can lead to misunderstandings between persons at the work place.
- **Different Values:** Workplace is made up of individuals who see the world differently. Conflict occurs when people do not accept and understand these differences.
- **Differing Interests:** Conflict occurs when individual workers forget the organisational goals and put forth their personal goals.
- **Scarce Resources:** This world is not blessed with plenty of resources. In a resource scarce world like this, conflicts arise because everyone wants to have his maximum share.
- **Personality Clashes:** All work environments are made up of differing personalities. Unless colleagues understand and accept each other's approach to work and problem-solving, conflict will occur.
- **Poor Performance:** when one or more individuals within a work unit are not performing - not working up to potential – and this is not addressed, conflict is inevitable.

> The quality of our lives depends not on whether or not we have conflicts, but on how we respond to them.
> – Tom Crum

Common reactions to Conflict:

Pretend the problem does not exist

People pretend as if there is no problem at all. Avoiding the problem will not make it go away

Blame someone else

People have the tendency to put the blame on others. Criticizing the other person or starting a rumor about someone else will not make the problem go away

Try to start a fight

People indulging in quarrel, argument or fight over a conflict. Calling someone a name, being physically violent, or being very sarcastic will not make the problem go away

> Don't look where you fall, but where you slipped.
> – African proverb

In short we respond to conflict in the following ways

Emotional responses

These are the feelings we experience in conflict, ranging from anger and fear to despair and confusion. Emotional responses are often misunderstood, as people tend to believe that others feel the same as they do. Thus, differing emotional responses are confusing and, at times, threatening.

Cognitive responses

These are our ideas and thoughts about a conflict, often present as inner voices or internal observers in the midst of a situation. Through sub-vocalization (i.e., self-talk), we come to understand these cognitive responses. For example, we might think any of the following things in response to another person taking a parking spot just as we are ready to park:

Physical responses:

These responses can play an important role in our ability to meet our needs in the conflict. They include heightened stress, bodily tension, increased perspiration, tunnel vision, shallow or accelerated breathing, nausea, and rapid heartbeat. These responses are similar to those we experience in high-anxiety situations, and they may be managed through stress management techniques.

> A problem is your chance to do your best.
>
> – Duke Ellington

Functional aspects of conflict

- Increased group performance
- Improved quality of decisions
- Stimulation of creativity and innovation
- Encouragement of interest and curiosity
- Provision of a medium for problem-solving
- Creation of an environment for self-evaluation and change

> In the middle of difficulty lies opportunity.
>
> – Albert Einstein

Dysfunctional aspects of conflict

- Development of discontent
- Reduced group effectiveness
- Retarded communication
- Reduced group cohesiveness
- Infighting among group members overcomes group goals

Conflict Management Vs Conflict Resolution

Conflict management refers to the long-term management of intractable conflicts. It involves implementing strategies to limit the negative aspects of conflict and to increase the positive aspects of conflict at a level equal to or higher than where the conflict is taking place. Furthermore, the aim of conflict management is to enhance learning and group outcomes.

"Conflict management involves designing effective macro-level strategies to minimize the dysfunctions of conflict.

> Forgiveness does not change the past, but it does enlarge the future.
> – Paul Boese

Meaning of conflict resolution

Conflict resolution is a wide range of methods of addressing sources of conflict - whether at the inter-personal level or between states - and of finding means of resolving a given conflict or of continuing it in less destructive forms than, say, armed conflict.

It is a process of ending a disagreement between two or more people in a constructive fashion for all parties involved.

It is an intervention aimed at alleviating or eliminating discord through conciliation.

As the name would suggest, conflict resolution involves the reduction, elimination, or termination of all forms and types of conflict. In practice, when people talk about conflict resolution they tend to use terms like negotiation, bargaining, mediation, or arbitration.

In line with the recommendations in the "how to" section, businesses can benefit from appropriate types and levels of conflict. That is the aim of conflict management, and not the aim of conflict resolution.

> Don't find fault. Find a remedy.
> - Henry Ford

Ways of addressing conflict

Five basic ways of addressing conflict were identified by Thomas and Kilmann

- **Avoidance** – This style indicates that people try to evade the conflict entirely. This style represents delegating controversial decisions, accepting default decisions, and not wanting to hurt anyone's feelings. It can be appropriate when victory is impossible, when the controversy is trivial, or when someone else is in a better position to solve the problem. However in many situations this is a weak and ineffective approach to take.
- In other words this method means, avoid or postpone conflict by ignoring it, changing the subject, etc. Avoidance can be useful as a temporary measure to buy time or as an expedient means of dealing with very minor, non-recurring conflicts. In more severe cases, conflict avoidance can involve severing a relationship or leaving a group.
- **Accommodation** – This style indicates a willingness to meet the needs of others at the expense of the person's own needs. This person is not assertive but is highly cooperative. Accommodation is appropriate when peace is more valuable than winning, or when you want to be in a position to collect on this favour you gave. However people may not return favours, and overall this approach is unlikely to give the best outcomes.
- In other words, this method means surrendering one's own needs and wishes to accommodate the other party.
- **Competition** – This style indicate that people take a firm stand, and know what they want. They usually operate from a position of power, drawn from things like position, rank, expertise, or persuasive ability. This style can be useful when there is an emergency and a decision needs to be make fast; when the

decision is unpopular; or when defending against someone who is trying to exploit the situation selfishly. However it can leave people feeling bruised, unsatisfied and resentful when used in less urgent situations. It can be useful when achieving one's objectives outweighs one's concern for the relationship.

- In other words, competition means assert one's viewpoint at the potential expense of another.

> Don't ever take a fence down until you know why it was put up.
> – Robert Frost

- **Compromise** – This style indicates that people try to find a solution that will at least partially satisfy everyone. Everyone is expected to give up something and the compromiser him- or herself also expects to relinquish something. Compromise is useful when the cost of conflict is higher than the cost of losing ground. The aim of conflict resolution is to reach agreement and most often this will mean compromise.
- In other words this method means bring the problem into the open and have the third person present.
- **Collaboration** – This style indicates that people try to meet the needs of all people involved. These people can be highly assertive but unlike the competitor, they cooperate effectively and acknowledge that everyone is important. This style is useful when you need to bring together a variety of viewpoints to get the best solution; when there have been previous conflicts in the group; or when the situation is too important for a simple trade-off.
- In other words, collaboration means, work together to find a mutually beneficial solution. collaboration can also be time-intensive and inappropriate when there is not enough trust, respect or communication among participants for collaboration to occur. While the Thomas-Kilmann grid views collaboration as the only win-win solution to conflict.

> You can't shake hands with a clenched fist.
> – Indira Gandhi

The Dual Concern Model of the Styles of Handling Interpersonal Conflict

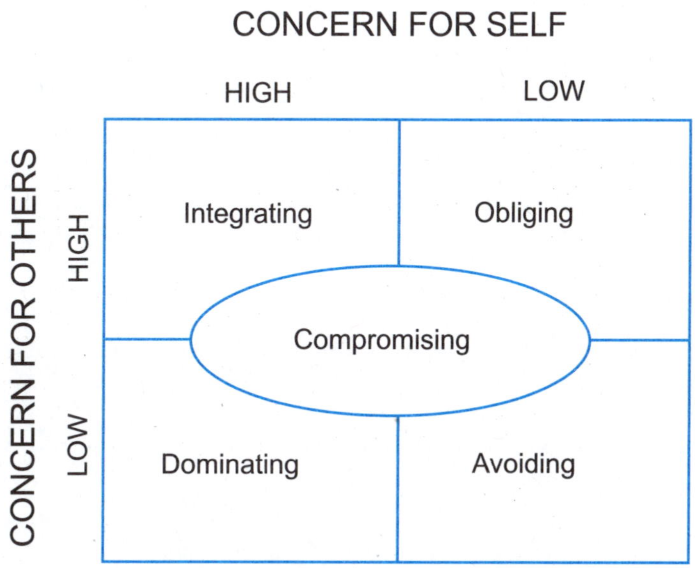

Styles of Handling Interpersonal Conflict and the Situations Where They are appropriate or Inappropriate

Conflict Style	Situations where appropriate	Situations where inappropriate
Integrating	1. Issues are complex 2. Synthesis of ideas is needed to come up with better solutions. 3. Commitment is needed from other parties for successful implementation. 4. Time is available for problem solving. 5. One party alone cannot solve the problem. 6. Resources possessed by different parties are needed to solve their common problems.	1. Task or problem is simple. 2. Immediate decision is required. 3. Other parties are unconcerned about outcome. 4. Other parties do not have problem solving skills.
Obliging	1. You believe that you may be wrong. 2. Issue is more important to the other party. 3. You are willing to give up something in exchange for something from the other party in the future. 4. You are dealing from a position of weakness. 5. Preserving relationship is important	1. Issue is important to you 2. You believe that you are right. 3. The other party is wrong or unethical.
Dominating	1. Issue is trivial 2. Speedy decision is needed. 3. Unpopular course of action is implemented 4. Necessary to overcome assertive subordinates. 5. Unfavourable decision by the other party may be costly to you. 6. Subordinates lack experties to make technical decisions. 7. Issue is important to you.	1. Issue is complex. 2. Issue is not important to you. 3. Both parties are equally powerful. 4. Decision does not have to be made quickly. 5. Subordinates possess high degree of competence.
Avoiding	1. Issue is trivial 2. Potential dysfunctional effect of confronting the other party outweighs benefits of resolution. 3. Cooling off period is needed.	1. Issue is important to you. 2. It is your responsibility to make decision. 3. Parties are unwilling to defer, issue must be resolved. 4. Prompt attention is needed.
Compromising	1. Goals of parties are mutually exclusive. 2. Parties are equally powerful. 3. Consensus cannot be reached. 4. Integrating or dominating style is not successful. 5. Temporary solution to a complex problem is needed.	1. One party is more powerful 2. Problem is complex enough needing problem-solving approach

Managing conflict

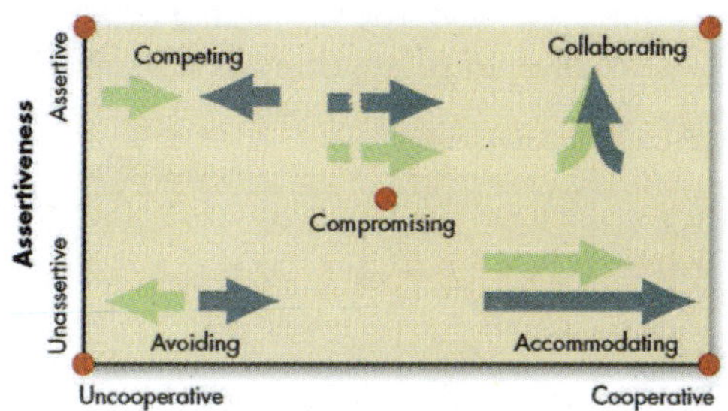

When conflict is mismanaged, it can harm the relationship. But when handled in a positive way, conflict provides an opportunity for growth. By learning the skills you need for successful conflict resolution, you can face disagreements with confidence and keep your personal and professional relationships strong and growing.

> Nothing can bring you peace but yourself. – Ralph Waldo Emerson

How to handle the silent treatment

- Allow them to be silent for a while if necessary, be patient
- Does the person prefer to speak in private? If needs be, use an external arbitrator or bring in a counsellor
- Encourage discussion by using open-ended questions
- Rephrase difficult questions

How to handle the gossips

- Get them to acknowledge whether they are describing assumed versus evidenced behavior
- Keep an open mind and get corroboration if needed
- Keep questions closed
- Remind the person that you only need to know facts and their own feelings

How to handle the non-stop talkers

- Ask them to sum up feelings using keywords
- Control the flow, interrupt kindly but firmly
- Get them to list issues in bullet point
- Keep questions closed
- Set a time for them to talk more about the issue at a later date, or set up a session with a counsellor

> Every fight is on some level a fight between differing 'angles of vision' illuminating the same truth.
> – Gandhi

How to handle interruptions

- If they constantly interrupt, consider communicating with each party separately
- Remind the person interrupting that they will get their chance to speak
- Request cooperation and respect
- Use non-verbal statements such as facial expression
- Have the person removed from site if necessary, using security officers or equivalent.
- Immediately request the behaviour stops and explain why it is unacceptable
- Pause or end the meeting
- Remove the person/s to a safe environment and allow them to cool down

> Never ruin an apology with an excuse.
> – Kimberly Johnson

When a situation has progressed to crisis stage

In this scenario, the only option is to manage the crisis situation as best as you can in the circumstances. The aim of crisis management is to return the work environment to some semblance of normality, calm tempers and prevent violent or unacceptable acts of behaviour from occurring.

How to handle high emotions

- Allow the person time to compose themselves, if necessary give them a cool down period in a safe environment

- Be calm and supportive
- Bring in a counsellor if necessary.
- Does the person prefer to speak in private?

> Anger is an acid that can do more harm to the vessel in which it stands than to anything on which it is poured.
>
> – Gandhi

How to handle anger

- Be patient
- Prevent the anger from being focused on the other party
- Request respect and cooperation
- Stay calm and in control – your calmness will help diffuse their anger

> Our task is not to fix blame for the past, but to fix the course for the future.
>
> – John F. Kennedy

Healthy and unhealthy ways of managing and resolving conflict

	Unhealthy responses to conflict:	•	Healthy responses to conflict
•	An inability to recognize and respond to the things that matter to the other person	•	The capacity to recognize and respond to the things that matter to the other person
•	Explosive, angry, hurtful, and resentful reactions	•	Calm, non-defensive, and respectful reactions
•	The withdrawal of love, resulting in rejection, isolation, shaming, and fear of abandonment	•	A readiness to forgive and forget, and to move past the conflict without holding resentments or anger
•	An inability to compromise or see the other person's side.	•	The ability to seek compromise and avoid punishing
•	The fear and avoidance of conflict; the expectation of bad outcomes	•	A belief that facing conflict head is the best thing for both sides

Steps for conflict resolution

1. Know Yourself

Self-awareness and care are essential to an effective approach to conflict management. The more you are aware of your biases and "hot buttons," the more likely you can prepare yourself mentally, emotionally and physically to respond in a preferred way.

2. Clarify Needs Threatened by the conflict

Substantive needs are the ones that are directly related to the conflict.

Procedural needs relate to the process adopted to solve the aforesaid conflict. Namely they refer to the ground rules deployed to solve the conflict.

Psychological needs relate to personal feelings and sentiments of the people involved.

3. Identify a proper Place for Negotiation

Identify a private, neutral room to hold your conversation. If the conversation starts in a more public place it may affect the discussion.

4. Develop taste for listening

If you dedicate to active listening, you can improve the likelihood that your ideas and feelings will be understood by the other person. And if you truly come to understand the other's point of view in the conflict, you may be able to understand why the problem has reached this stage.

> What we see depends mainly on what we look for.
> – Sir John Lubbock

5. Assert Your Needs

At this point, it is important to get your views communicated as clearly as possible. Assertive communication is the process of conveying one's needs and concerns clearly while respecting the needs of the other party. It may be contrasted to aggressive communication, where one conveys needs globally and without respectful listening, or submissive communication, where one vaguely conveys needs in a manner that is often confusing to the listener.

6. Be flexible

Generate several possible solutions to the problem by holding brainstorming sessions. Develop an open mind to generate more than one ideas. It is useful to explore a few additional ideas before settling on the best answer to the problem.

7. Handle Impasse with Calm and Respect

Impasse is the point within a dispute in which the parties are unable to reach effective solutions. People feel stuck, frustrated, angry, and disillusioned. As a result, they may turn hostile or walk out. In any case, impasse represents a turning point in your efforts to negotiate a solution to the conflict. As such, rather than avoiding it, impasse should be seen with calm, patience, and respect.

> There is no way to peace. Peace is the way. – A. J. Muste

8. Build an Agreement that Works

As you come to the conclusion of the negotiation process, identify areas of agreement clearly and preferably in writing. Then review the agreement in light of the organisation and its policies.

9. Focus on the present.

If you're holding on to old hurts and resentments, your ability to see the reality of the current situation will be impaired. Rather than looking to the past and assigning blame, focus on what you can do in the here-and-now to solve the problem.

10. Be willing to forgive.

Resolving conflict is impossible if you're unwilling or unable to forgive. Resolution lies in releasing the urge to punish, which can never compensate for our losses and only adds to our injury by further depleting and draining our lives.

11. Know when to let something go

If you can't come to an agreement, agree to disagree. It takes two people to keep an argument going. If a conflict is going nowhere, you can choose to disengage and move on.

> The more we sweat in peace the less we bleed in war.
> – Vijaya Lakshmi Pandit

Steps for on-line conflict resolution

1. Set a time and place for discussion

In most cases blogging conflict happens in posts and comments between bloggers. If a comment thread is becoming destructive take the discussion to a more private setting either via email or IM. Setting up a discussion for some point in the future helps to give each party a little space to calm down and approach the interaction more reasonably.

2. Define the problem

Many online conflicts tend to spill out into related topics to the point where parties end up not really knowing what they're fighting

SIX STEPS IN THE CONFLECT RESOLUTION PROCESS

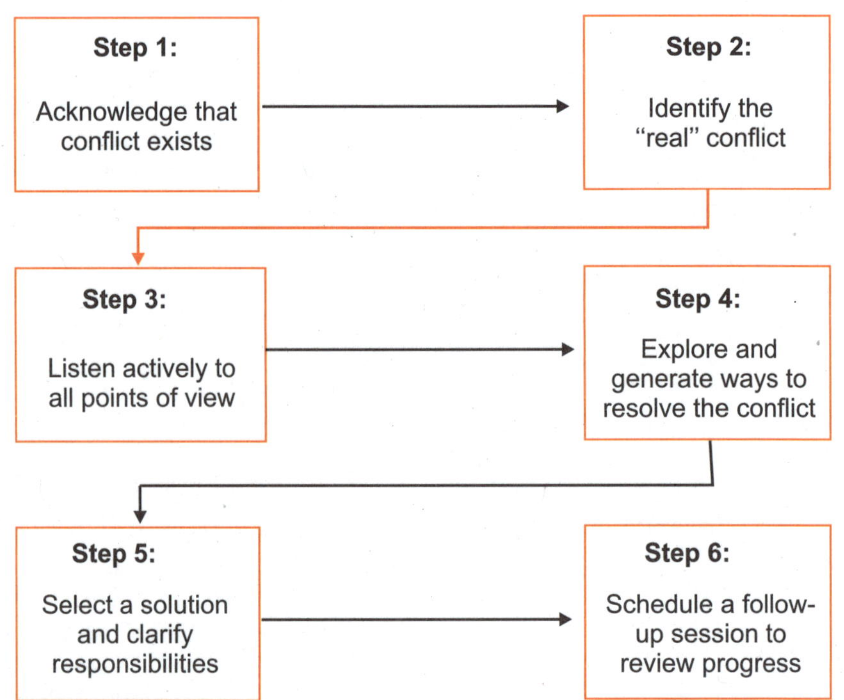

about at all. Attempting to keep a discussion to one main point (at a time) can mean you're more likely to move through it and then tackle another issue.

> Discussion is an exchange of knowledge; argument an exchange of emotion.
> – Robert Quillen

3. Try to find the mistakes committed by you

Conflict is rarely a result of one person solely being at fault in a situation. Communicating to each other not only what the other person has done wrong but identifying your own failings can be a humbling experience and usually brings you a long way closer to resolving the issue.

4. List past attempts to resolve the issue that were not successful

As blogging conflicts don't usually come out of longer term relationships this might not be as relevant. However there are occasions where the same issues surface again and again and it can be helpful to identify previous occasions and look at what the resolution was.

5. List all possible solutions

When people fight they generally push one argument or solution upon others and are not willing to entertain the idea that there might be other possible solutions. Listing the alternative opinions and solutions can help both parties to find compromise.

> It takes two to quarrel, but only one to end it. – Spanish Proverb

6. Discuss and evaluate these possible solutions

Talking over the alternatives in a neutral and objective way helps both parties to see the pros and cons of different ways of thinking.

7. Agree on one solution to try

In some cases there is no 'solution' needed either to agree to disagree and to move on. However in some cases there might be more. Agreeing how and when to finish the conflict is important and stops those lingering flame wars where neither party is willing to let the other one have the final word.

8. Agree on how each individual will work toward this solution

If there's some sort of agreement on the resolution to agree to how each person will contribute to it is important so that there is accountability around it.

> The first problem for all of us, men and women, is not to learn, but to unlearn. – Gloria Steinem

9. Set up another meeting. Discuss your progress

When you have a blog conflict with someone and have moved to some point of resolution that it can be helpful to privately contact the person later on to debrief on it and to see if there is any further resolution needed.

10. Reward each other as each contribute toward the solution

Positive affirmation goes a long way in all types of relationships and in blogging it's just as important.

Once again, it takes a commitment to all parties involved to move through conflict in a positive way.

Books for further reading

- Resolving Conflicts at Work: Ten Strategies for Everyone on the Job, Kenneth Cloke and Joan Goldsmith, Jossey-Bass; 3 editions, May 24, 2011.
- Conflict Resolution, Daniel Dana, McGraw-Hill; 1 edition (December 13, 2000).

- The Eight Essential Steps to Conflict Resolution, Dudley Weeks, Tarcher; First Edition, January 4, 1994.
- Communication and Conflict Resolution Skills, KATZ NEIL H et al, Kendall Hunt Publishing; 2 edition, May 13, 2011.
- Interpersonal Conflict, William Wilmot and Joyce Hocker, McGraw-Hill Humanities/Social Sciences/Languages; 8 edition .January 12, 2010.
- Conflict Resolution: Theory, Research, and Practice, James A. Schellenberg, SUNY Press, 1974.
- Conflict Resolution: Mediation Tools for Everyday Work life, Daniel Dana, McGrawhill Professional, 2001.
- Contemporary Conflict Resolution, Oliver Ramsbotham, Tom Woodhouse, Hugh Miall, Polity Press, 1988.
- Conflict Resolution: Communication, Cooperation, Compromise, Robert Wandberg, Capstone Press, 2000.
- Managing Conflict through Communication (4th Edition), Ruth Anna Abigail and Dudley D. Cahn, Allyn & Bacon; January 13, 2010.
- The Conflict Resolution Toolbox: Models and Maps for Analyzing, Diagnosing, Gary T. Furlong, John Wiley & Sons, 2005.
- Conflict Resolved?: A Critical Assessment of Conflict Resolution, Alan Tidwell, Continnum International Publishing, 1998.
- Conflict resolution: dynamics, process and structure, Ho-Won Jeong, Ashgate, 1999.
- Conflict: From Analysis to Intervention, Sandra Cheldelin, Daniel Druckman, Larissa A. Fast, Continuum International Publishing Group, 01-Aug-2003.

12 Team Building and Teamwork

LEARNING OUTCOME

- Meaning
- Aspects of team building
- Skills needed for teamwork
- A model of team building
- Team Vs Group
- Characteristics of effective team
- Role of a team leader
- Role of team members
- Nine persons a successful team should have
- Inter-group collaboration
- Advantages of inter-group collaboration
- Difficulties faced in inter-group collaboration
- Factors shaping inter-group collaboration
- Exercise : Test your teamwork skills

Together
Everyone
Achieves
More

Introduction

Today's world is driven by innovation leading to constant change and success of an organization depends on its teams. Thus it has become mandatory to train the employees in all spheres of management. Team building is one of the crucial areas in which the employees are to be trained.

Effective teams are necessary for the continual growth, development and management of an organization. The success of an organization depends on the kinds of team it has. Projects require people to work together, so teamwork has become an important concept in organizations. Effective teams are an intermediary towards getting good, sustainable results. Industry has seen increasing efforts through training and cross-training to help people to work together more effectively and to accomplish common goals.

Teamwork is the concept of people working together cooperatively as in a sports team.

"The old structures are being reformed. As organizations seek to become more flexible in the face of LPG(Liberalisation, Privatisation, Globalisation) they are experimenting with new, team-based structures".

A survey recently conducted revealed that 'being a team player' was the most important factor in getting ahead in the workplace. This was ranked higher than several factors, including 'merit and performance', 'leadership skills', 'intelligence', and 'making money for the organization'.

Meaning

"A team is a small group of people with complementary skills and abilities who are committed to a common goal and approach for which they hold each other accountable."

- Team is a group of people working towards a common objective.
- Teamwork is the concept of people working together cooperatively.
- Teamwork is something like synergy where the whole is greater that the parts.

Aspects of team building

A popular theory of Carron defines four different areas of interest:

- Team Identity
- Team Structure
- Team Goals
- Team Motivation

Team identity

This is important. Everybody wants to be a part of the group. People identify themselves with the social groups. Think about:

- Organise trips, training weekends, etc.
- A unique name for your team
- A special kit, logo, etc.
- Remember your players of the history of the team
- Install some pride in what the team is doing

Team structure

Within each team you can define clear roles. Most of them are of course related to the traditional positions. First is role clarity, every player knows what to do in every situation (this is sometimes difficult to define so give your players a sort of minimum requirements list). Second, is the acceptance of the role. Each player should feel comfortable in the position he is playing. Last is the performance of the player in the role.

Team goals

- Help the team to set themselves clear and realistic goals.
- Make the players understand that they need to adhere to team standards, each individual player shares responsibility for the success of the team.
- Give the individual players and the team as a whole feedback on their progress.
- Accept no rivalry, encourage co-operation.

Team motivation

- When you can meet the individual needs of players, those players will be motivated to achieve. Do you know why your players play the game?
- Ask for sacrifices for the team, loyalty towards each other.
- Install a sense of responsibility in the players.
- Make a check-list on these above items and set up a strategy to work on each separate topic.

Skills needed for teamwork

Besides technical proficiency you need to have a wide variety of social skills desired for successful teamwork. They are

✶ Listening

It is important to listen to other people's ideas. Where ideas are freely expressed they pave way for the other ideas to emerge.

✶ Questioning

It is important to ask questions, interact and discuss the objectives of the team.

✶ Persuading

It is important to exchange, defend, rethink and if needed change the ideas.

✶ Respecting

It is essential to treat others ideas and views with respect and accept when they prove worth.

✶ Helping

It is the core principle in teamwork.

✶ Sharing

Sharing creates a conducive environment for the team to work.

✶ Participating

It makes the work easier and simple.

✶ Communication

To work effectively in a team you have to acquire good communication skills.

A model of team building

Team building process

★ Forming

This is a process of getting members acquainted with one another and start feeling themselves as part of a group.

In the first stages of team building, the *forming* of the team takes place. The team meets and learns about the opportunity and challenges, and then agrees on goals and begins to tackle the tasks.

The forming stage of any team is important because in this stage the members of the team get to know one another and make new friends. This is also a good opportunity to see how each member of the team works as an individual and how they respond to pressure.

★ Storming

This is a process of conflict, confrontation, concern and criticism. Members question each other's intention. But at the end, the members come together towards achieving group task.

- Every group will then enter the *storming* stage in which different ideas compete for consideration. The team addresses issues such as what problems they are really supposed to solve, how they will function independently and together and what leadership model they will accept. Team members open up to each other and confront each other's ideas and perspectives.
- In some cases *storming* can be resolved quickly. In others, the team never leaves this stage. The maturity of some team members usually determines whether the team will ever move out of this stage. Immature team members will begin acting out to demonstrate how much they know and convince others that their ideas are correct. Some team members will focus on minutiae to evade real issues.
- The *storming* stage is necessary to the growth of the team. It can be contentious, unpleasant and even painful to members of the team who are averse to conflict. Tolerance of each team member and their differences needs to be emphasized. Without tolerance and patience the team will fail. This phase can become destructive to the team and will lower motivation if allowed to get out of control.

✦ Norming

This is a process of developing close relationship among the members. The group experiences cohesiveness.

- At some point, the team may enter the *norming* stage. Team members adjust their behaviour to each other as they develop work habits that make teamwork seem more natural and fluid. Team members often work through this stage by agreeing on rules, values, professional behaviour, shared methods, working tools and even taboos. During this phase, team members begin to trust each other. Motivation increases as the team gets more acquainted with the project.
- Teams in this phase may lose their creativity if the norming behaviours become too strong and begin to stifle healthy dissent and the team begins to exhibit groupthink.

✦ Performing

This is a stage of developing high level maturity. The group experiences teamwork, clarity, and task accomplishment.

Some teams will reach the *performing* stage. These high-performing teams are able to function as a unit as they find ways to get the job done smoothly and effectively without inappropriate conflict or the need for external supervision. Team members have become interdependent. By this time they are motivated and knowledgeable. The team members are now competent, autonomous and able to handle the decision-making process without supervision. Dissent is expected and allowed as long as it is channeled through means acceptable to the team.

✦ Adjourning

This is a stage of separation. The members of the group are separated for two reasons. The group might have completed its task or the members decide to close the group.

- Tuckman later added a fifth phase, *adjourning*, that involves completing the task and breaking up the team. Others call it the phase for *mourning*.
- A team that lasts may transcend to a *transforming* phase of achievement. *Transformational management* can produce major changes in performance through synergy and is considered to be more far-reaching than transactional management.

Team *VS* Group

Many people used the words team and group interchangeably, but there are actually a number of differences between a team and a group in real world applications. Here are some differences.

1. Understanding

In a group, members think they are grouped together for administrative purposes only. Individuals sometimes cross purpose with others.

In a team, members recognise their independence and understand both personal and team goals are best accomplished with mutual support. Time is not wasted struggling or attempting personal gain at the expense of others.

2. Ownership

In a group, members tend to focus on themselves because they are not sufficiently involved in planning the unit's objectives. They approach their job simply as a hired hand. "Castle Building" is common.

In a team, members feel a sense of ownership for their jobs and unit, because they are committed to values based on common goals.

3. Creativity and contribution

In a group, members are told what to do rather than being asked what the best approach would be. Suggestions and creativity are not encouraged.

In a team, members contribute to the organisation's success by applying their unique talents, knowledge and creativity to team objectives.

4. Trust

In a group, members distrust the motives of colleagues because they do not understand the role of other members. Expressions of opinion or disagreement are considered divisive or non-supportive.

In a team, members work in a climate of trust and are encouraged to openly express ideas, opinions, disagreements and feelings.

5. Common understandings

In a group, members are so cautious

about what they say, that real understanding is not possible. Game playing may occur and communication traps be set to catch the defaulters.

In a team, members practice open and honest communication. They make an effort to understand each others' point of view.

6. Personal development

In a group, members receive good training but are limited in applying it to the job by the manager or other group members.

In a team, members are encouraged to continually develop skills and apply what they learn on the job. They perceive they have the support of the team.

7. Conflict resolution

In a group, members find themselves in conflict situations they do not know how to resolve. Their supervisor/leader may put off intervention until serious damage is done.

In a team, members realise conflict is a normal aspect of human interaction but they view such situations as an opportunity for new ideas and creativity. They work to resolve conflicts quickly and constructively.

8. Participative decision making

In a group, members may or may not participate in decisions affecting the team. Conformity often appears more important than positive results. Win/lose situations are common.

In a team, members participate in decisions affecting the team but understand their leader must make a final ruling whenever the team cannot decide, or an emergency exists. Positive win/win results are the goal at all times.

9. Clear leadership

In a group, members tend to work in an unstructured environment with undetermined standards of performance. Leaders do not walk the talk and tend to lead from behind a desk.

In a team, members work in a structured environment, they know what boundaries exist and who has final authority. The leader sets agreed high standards of performance and he/she is respected via active, willing participation.

10. Commitment

In a group, members are uncommitted towards excellence and personal pride. Performance levels tend to be mediocre. Staff turnover is high because talented individuals quickly recognise that (a) personal expectations are not being fulfilled, (b) they are not learning and growing from others and (c) they are not working with the best people.

In a team, only those committed to excellence are hired. Prospective team members are queuing at the door to be recruited on the basis of their high levels of hard and soft skill sets. Everyone works together in a harmonious environment.

Characteristics of effective team

- ✓ Friendly
- ✓ Interested
- ✓ Listen to others
- ✓ Recognize and reward
- ✓ Leadership is rotated
- ✓ Decision by consensus
- ✓ Encourage and appreciate
- ✓ Committed to goals
- ✓ Spontaneous communication
- ✓ Open minded

Experience has demonstrated that successful teams are empowered to establish some or all of a team's goals, to make decisions about how to achieve these goals, to undertake the tasks required to meet them and to be mutually accountable for their results. There are several characteristics of an effective team. These include:

- **Clear Purpose** - The vision, mission, goal or task of the team has been defined and is now accepted by everyone. This is an action plan.
- **Informality** - The climate tends to be informal, comfortable and relaxed. There are no obvious tensions or signs of boredom.
- **Participation** - There is much discussion and everyone is encouraged to participate.
- **Listening** - The members use effective listening techniques such as questioning, paraphrasing and summarizing to get out ideas.
- **Civilized Disagreement** - If there is disagreement, the team must be comfortable with this and show no signs of avoiding, smoothing over or suppressing conflict.
- **Consensus Decisions** - For important decisions, the goal is substantial but not necessarily unanimous agreement through open discussion of everyone's ideas, avoidance of formal voting or easy compromises.
- **Open Communication** - Team members feel free to express their feelings on the tasks as well as on the group's operation. There are few hidden agendas. Communication takes place outside of meetings.
- **Clear Roles and Work Assignments** - There are clear expectations about the roles played by each team member. When action is taken, clear assignments are made, accepted and carried out. Work is fairly distributed among team members.
- **Shared Leadership** - While the team has a formal leader, leadership functions shift from time to time depending on the circumstances, the needs of the group and the skills of the members. The formal leader models the appropriate behaviour and helps establish positive norms.
- **External Relations** - The team spends time developing key relationships outside and mobilizing resources, then building credibility with important players in other parts of the organization.
- **Style Diversity** - The team has a broad spectrum of team-player types, including members who emphasize attention to task, goal setting, focus on process and questions about how the team is functioning.
- **Self-Assessment** - Periodically, the team stops to examine how well it is functioning and what may be interfering with its effectiveness.

Role of a team leader

Provide team leadership and coaching

- Create an environment oriented to trust, open communication, creative thinking, and cohesive team effort.
- Provide the team with a vision of the project objectives.
- Motivate and inspire team members.
- Lead by setting a good example (role model) - behaviour consistent with words.
- Coach and help develop team members; help resolve dysfunctional behaviour.
- Facilitate problem solving and collaboration.
- Strive for team consensus and win-win agreements.

- Maintain healthy group dynamics.
- Intervene when necessary to aid the group in resolving issues.
- Assure that the team members have the necessary education and training to effectively participate in the team.
- Encourage creativity, risk-taking, and constant improvement.
- Recognize and celebrate team and team member accomplishments and exceptional performance.

Focus the team on the tasks at hand

- Coordinate with internal and external customers as necessary.
- Familiarize the team with the customer needs and specifications to support task performance.
- Assure that the team addresses all relevant issues within the specifications and various standards.
- Provide necessary business information.
- Serve as meeting manager or chairman.
- Ensure deliverables are prepared to satisfy the project requirements, cost and schedule.
- Help keep the team focused and on track.

Coordinate team logistics

- Work with functional managers and the team sponsor to obtain necessary resources to support the team's requirements.
- Obtain and coordinate space, furniture, equipment, and communication lines for team members.
- Establish meeting times, places and agendas.
- Coordinate the review, presentation and release of design layouts, drawings, analysis and other documentation.
- Coordinate meetings with the product committee, project manager and functional management to discuss project impediments, needed resources or issues/delays in completing the task.

Communicate

- Provide status reporting of team activities against the programme plan or schedule
- Keep the project manager and product committee informed of task accomplishment, issues and status.
- Serve as a focal point to communicate and resolve interface and integration issues with other teams.
- Escalate issues which cannot be resolved by the team.
- Provide guidance to the team based on management direction.

> "The strength of a wolf lies in his group".

Team leader should not merely have requisite knowledge and skills but also play his role in a manner that facilitates team building.

- ❖ Establishing clear aims
- ❖ Starting the process in a modest way
- ❖ Communicating the concept
- ❖ Ensuring agreement
- ❖ Building realistic time schedule
- ❖ Consulting widely and genuinely

Role of team members

1. Care for each other

The teams that are most effective care about each other. They have a genuine interest in each other and their success and fulfillment. Think about times when things were going really well in a group. More than likely one of the most powerful things that was pulling the team together was genuine interest in each other.

2. Open and truthful

Openness and truthfulness is the second key characteristic of effective teams. When teams are open and truthful, they step forward, say things that need to be said, all in the interest of helping the team to get results.

3. High levels of trust

Teams that are looking over their shoulder all of the time, who worry about what is being said in smaller groups, who don't believe they can rely on others and are looking to points score will not create high levels of trust. If there are low levels of trust, it is extremely difficult to excel as a team.

4. Consensus decisions

If you are someone who looks at decisions through a lens of getting what you want and this is replicated across a team, how effective do you think that team would be? Consensus decision making is not about avoiding taking decisions or watering down decisions. It is about looking for the best win-win outcome for the team.

5. Commitment

The teams that are effective are committed to getting the results they desire. They know where they are heading, are highly motivated and persistent even when setbacks arise. Commitment in many ways is about doing what it takes to get the result you want.

6. Address conflict

Sometimes people wrongly believe that in effective teams there is no conflict. The difference between those teams that excel and those that struggle is that conflict is addressed. Rather than seeing it as something negative, teams recognise it as healthy and to be worked through in order to get the desired results.

7. Real listening

Listening is the key to effective communication and effective teams know that it is important to really listen and understand. Real listening is about focusing attention on the communicator rather than your own personal agenda. Teams who only master this will go a long way to being more effective.

8. Express feelings

We are often told to keep emotions and feelings out of the workplace. Yet in truth, if teams want to be effective they need to create a safe and courageous space for feelings to be expressed. Think about an investment decision.

It is equally important for the team members to ensure the following :

- Be clear about the objectives of the team
- Identify individual skills
- Reflect the work methods
- Set targets for improvement
- Develop close relationship
- Have an open relationship

Nine persons a successful team should have

1. **Coordinator:** This person will have a clear view of the team's objectives and is skilled at extracting work from others.
2. **Shaper:** This person will make things happen and get things going. This person tries to pull things together.
3. **Planner:** This person is the one who is most likely to come out with original ideas and challenges the traditional ones. This person provides major insights and ideas for changes.
4. **Resource investigator:** This person with his strong contacts and networks, brings lot of information and support from outside. This person is enthusiastic in pursuit of the team's goals.
5. **Implementer:** This person is well organized and effective at turning big ideas into manageable tasks. This person is logical, methodical but experience flexibility.
6. **Completer:** This person is the one who reaches the deadlines and targets. This person is time conscious and effective at checking.
7. **Evaluator:** This person is good at evaluating all options. He/She can judge the situations accurately.
8. **Specialist:** This person provides specialist skills and knowledge. He/She has a single-minded approach to reach the target.
9. **Finisher:** This is a person who sticks to deadlines and likes to get on with things. He/She is someone who doesn't believe in relaxing at workplace.

Inter-group collaboration

Working across groups can be challenging because you have to rely on people from other groups who have different priorities than your own. If you are a manager, you have no direct authority over the other group. When cross-group work breaks down, it works two ways, either you put the blame on others or others put the blame on you.

Advantages of inter-group collaboration

1. Time and money saved
2. Increased customer satisfaction
3. Decreased redundancy by clarifying work
4. Increased diversity and creative solutions
5. Opportunities for career development

Difficulties faced in inter-group collaboration

1. Resistance to change
2. Different groups
3. Competing goals between groups.

4. Limited resources (time, money, people)
5. Corporate structures
6. Communication problems
7. Getting appropriate sponsorship from upper management

Factors shaping inter-group collaboration

1. Goals/Values
2. Hierarchy/power
3. Communication pattern
4. History of the organizations
5. Unique complexities

EXERCISE

Test Your Teamwork Skills

Answer the following about how you would respond within a team

Very frequently	Frequently
5	4
Sometimes	Rarely
3	2

Never

1

1. I offer opinion and information

   5 4 3 2 1

2. I summarize what is happening in the group

   5 4 3 2 1

3. When there is a problem I try to identify what is happening

   5 4 3 2 1

4. I start the group working

   5 4 3 2 1

5. I suggest directions the group can take

   5 4 3 2 1

6. I listen actively

   5 4 3 2 1

7. I give positive feedback to other members of the group

   5 4 3 2 1

8. I compromise

   5 4 3 2 1

9. I help relieve tension

   5 4 3 2 1

10. I talk

    5 4 3 2 1

11. I ensure that meeting times and places are arranged

    5 4 3 2 1

12. I try to observe what is happening in the group

    5 4 3 2 1

13. I try to help solve the problem

    5 4 3 2 1

14. I take responsibility for ensuring that tasks are completed

    5 4 3 2 1

15. I like the group to have a good time

    5 4 3 2 1

Books for Further Reading

- (Group Interaction in High Risk Environments. Burlington, VT: *Ashgate Pub.*, 2004.
- Duarte, Deborah L., and Nancy Tennant Snyder. Mastering Virtual Teams: Strategies, Tools, and Techniques That Succeed. San Francisco, CA: Jossey-Bass, 2001.
- Fisher, Kimball. Leading Self-directed Work Teams: A Guide to Developing New Team Leadership Skills. New York, NY: McGraw-Hill, 2000.
- Katzenbach, Jon R. Teams at the Top: Unleashing the Potential of Both Teams and Individual Leaders. Boston, MA: Harvard Business School Press, 1998.
- Kinlaw, Dennis C. Superior Teams: What They Are and How to Develop Them. Brookfield, VT: Gower, 1998.
- Lewis, James P. Team-based Project Management. New York, NY: American Management Association, 1998.
- Love, Neil A., and Joan Brant-Love. The Project Sponsor Guide. Newtown Square, PA: Project Management Institute, 2000.
- Nash, Susan M. Turning Team Performance Inside Out: Team Types and Temperament for High-impact Results. Palo Alto, CA: Davies-Black Pub., 1999.
- Parker, Glenn M., Jerry McAdams, and David Zielinski. Rewarding teams: Lessons From the Trenches. San Francisco, CA: Jossey-Bass Publishers, 2001.
- United States. Workforce Compensation and Performance Service. Performance Appraisal for Teams: An Overview. Washington, DC: United States, Office of Personnel Management, Workforce Compensation and Performance Service, 1998.
- Adams, Susan, and Leda Kydoniefs. "Making Teams Work", Quality Progress, vol. XXXIII, no. I (Jan. 2000), p. 43-48.
- Apodaca, T., et al. Teamwork and Diversity: A Survey at Sandia National Laboratories. SAND—95-2427. Sandia National Labs., Albuquerque, NM, Nov. 1995.
- Arnwine, A.D. Are Self-Directed Work Teams Successful and Effective Tools for Today's Organization? Y/TS—1196. Oak Ridge National Lab., TN, 1 March 1995.
- Arterberrie, Rhonda Y., et al. Team Collaboration: Lessons Learned Report. NASA/TM—2005-213210. Glenn Research Center, Cleveland, OH, Jan. 2005.
- Ashby et al. "A' (A-PRIMED): A case study in teamwork", SAND—95-1303C, in 1995 Concurrent Engineering, Reston, VA, 23-25 Aug. 1995.
- Berman, M., et al. Principles and Guidelines for Diversity in Teamwork. SAND—94-1165. Sandia National Laboratories, Albuquerque, NM, Aug. 1994.
- Bolia, Robert S., and W. Todd Nelson. "Characterizing team performance in network-centric operations: philosophical and methodological issues", Aviation, Space, and Environmental Medicine, vol. LXXVIII, no. 5 Supp., p. 71-76.
- Cooper, Lynne P., Ann Majchrzak, and Samer Faraj. "Learning from project experiences using a legacy-based approach", in Hawaii International Conference on System Sciences, Kona, HI, 3 Jan. 2005.
- Department of Energy. Guide to Good Practices for Teamwork Training and Diagnostic Skills Development. DOE-HDBK—1202-97. USDOE Assistant Secretary for Environment, Safety, and Health, Washington, DC, 1 June 1997,

- Fischer, Ute, Lori McDonnell, and Judith Orasanu. "Linguistic correlates of team performance: toward a tool for monitoring team functioning during space missions", Aviation, Space, and Environmental Medicine, vol. LXXVIII, no. 5 Supp., p. 86-95.
- Frank, J.R. The Difference Between Teamwork and Compliance: The Application of Game Theory to Real-World Research Teams. ANL/ES/PP—82853. Argonne National Lab., IL, 1 April 1994.
- Garber, Russ, and M. Elisabeth Pate-Cornell. "Modeling the Effects of Dispersion of Design Teams on System Failure Risk", Journal of Spacecraft and Rockets, vol. XLI, no 1 (Jan./Feb. 2004), p. 60-68.
- Johnson, Michael D., et al. "Team Adaptation to Structural Misalignment: Determinants of Alternative Change Mechanisms", in Command and Control Research and Technology Symposium, San Diego, CA, 20-22 June 2006.
- Laske, M. and H. Neunteufel. "Why They Win or Lose (the Issue of Leadership in Virtual Project Teams)", in International Conference on Advances in the Internet, Processing, Systems, and Interdisciplinary research, Amalfi, Italy, 17-20 Feb. 2005.
- Lehtonen, Kenneth E. and Larry Barrett. "Managing a Product Development Team", Goddard Space Flight Center, Greenbelt, MD, Oct. 2003.
- Levine, John M., et al. Personnel Turnover and Team Performance. U.S. Army Research Institute for the Behavioral and Social Sciences, Arlington, VA, March 2005.
- Miller, M.A. Developing high-performance cross-functional teams: Understanding motivations, functional loyalties, and teaming fundamentals. LA—13120-T. Los Alamos National Lab., NM, 1 Aug. 1996.
- Sawyer, John E., et al. Development and Test of a Theory of Work Team Productivity. Air Force Research Laboratory, Mesa, AZ, July 2001.
- Shab, Ted. "XBoard: A Framework for Integrating and Enhancing Collaborative Work Practices", in SMC-IT 2006, Pasadena, CA, 17-21 July 2006.
- Wheeler, R., J. Hihn, J. and B. Wilkinson. "Distributed collaborative team effectiveness: measurement and process improvement", in Ninth International Society for Optical Engineering (SPIE) International Conference on Concurrent Engineering, Bedfordshire, UK, 27 July 2002.

Leadership Communication

LEARNING OUTCOME

- Defining Communication
- Importance of leadership communication
- Barriers to Communication
- Active Listening
- Feedback
- Non-verbal Behaviour of Communication
- Speaking Hints
- Communication mistakes
- Leadership Communication for Effective Teams
- Communicating effectively to the team
- Causes of poor leadership communication
- Principles of communication for having an effective team
- Books for further reading

> Talkers have always ruled. They will continue to rule. The smart thing is to join them." Bruce Barton

Communication these days is the buzz word. It gives you the ability to handle difficult times in organization. Today professionals have to compete globally and hence they have to be extra cautious while communicating. The different dimensions of communication can help them avoid conflict and confrontation. In a global world, we have to communicate globally to negotiate, to deal and to enable our discussion reach its desired destination.

The business world today needs leaders who should not only speak or write better but should also clarify, convince and come up with innovative ideas. An ill conceived thought, a poorly drafted correspondence, a hasty and clumsy report or an unorganized presentation can slacken the growth of organizations and individuals too. To a greater extent, your success as a leader/manager largely depends on your ability to communicate effectively with others. You should make an attempt to understand and be understood. if you look at any leader belonging to any country, starting from Winston Churchill to Barack Obama, you will find one common quality in them that is communication.

Effective leadership communication skills are a must in any leader. In the corporate world today, a leader communicates with a number of people on a daily basis, such as his subordinates, clients, media persons, shareholders, investors, etc. The success of any leader, in dealing, negotiating and working with all these people depends a lot on his interpersonal skills. If he is able to form a kind of connection with the people he interacts with, through his gestures, the way he communicates and presents himself, a leader is able to accomplish a lot more.

Defining Communication

Communication is the exchange and flow of information and ideas from one person to another; it involves a sender transmitting an idea, information, or feeling to a receiver. Effective communication occurs only if the receiver understands the exact information or idea that the sender intended to transmit. Many of the problems that occur in an organization are the either the direct result of people failing to communicate or processes, which leads to confusion. This confusion and process can cause good plans to fail.

Learning leadership communication skills requires that you practice and focus on learning it. Once you have learned and started practicing your leadership communication skills you will realize how much more efficient you can communicate with others.

> No one would talk much in the society if they knew how often they misunderstood others.
> –Johann Wolfgang Von Goethe

Importance of leadership communication

In the future managers will be chosen for their communication skills as much as their achievements. Front line managers have the greatest influence over managing their employees. Managers who are good communicators can keep the best workers focused, engaged, and productive. Managers who are good communicators get more from their direct reports than managers who have strong skills in other areas.

Contrary to what people believe, leadership communication skills can be acquired by anybody through practice. A thorough understanding of the psychology of the people leads to better communication. Anybody can inform his staff or clients about the company's products, policies, marketing strategies and other things, but it is up to the leader to transform mere information into effective communication.

> If you have nothing to say, say nothing.
>
> Mark Twain

Here are some ways in which leadership communication skills can be developed.

1. Open Communication

It is important as a leader to have good leadership communication skills and to allow an environment of open communication where the exchange of ideas, solutions, problems, can all be discussed without fear. A leader needs to communicate to subordinates that communication is important and ideas should be exchanged frequently. Open communication leads employees perform better, communicate better, and less problems will develop.

2. Clear Message

If you can develop the skill of sending clear messages, whether they are oral, non-verbal, or even written you can become an effective leader. There is less confusion when the leader sends clear messages because there is no room for misunderstandings. Learn this leadership skill and the misunderstandings will drop significantly in your organization.

3. Listen

To communicate effectively you also need to listen. By listening to your employees you will be able to actively handle any situations that arise long before they become problems. Also, you will know the needs of your employees, be better able to meet them, and as such be able to lead better.

And when your employees know you will listen to them they will be more likely to talk to you, which means your organization will be more successful when everyone is on the same page.

> You can have brilliant ideas, but if you can't get them across, your ideas won't get you anywhere.
>
> Lee Iacocca

4. Non-Verbal Behaviours

When you communicate with others you also need to know what tone of voice to use, facial expressions, and other gestures to exhibit good leadership communication skills. If you are saying something that is very important and serious to your organization, you need to have a serious face. If you are angry, you can convey this as well. Whatever is going on make sure your non-verbal behaviours coincide with what you are saying in order to communicate the most effective message.

5. Make Others Feel Special

How do great leaders became great. It is because all of them possess this great quality of connecting with people at some level, with the way they communicate. They have this uncanny ability to make people feel special through their leadership communication skills. And that's what differentiates successful leaders from others.

6. Inspirational

Every organization, whether political, social or economic, has a goal. There are some set of values, strategies and procedures, which every one working in it has to follow, in order to reach that goal. The leader should convey his and his organization's vision in a very clear and confident way so that people themselves take initiative in working towards that vision. A leader through his leadership qualities and communication, should be able to inspire other people to work for him.

7. Model the behaviour you are looking for from others

If a leader wants his staff to be transparent, respectful, trustworthy and open in their communication, he should model the same behaviour. After all leadership and their communication skills have a direct bearing on the way the subordinates behave and communicate.

> The art of communication is the language of leadership."
>
> James Humes

8.Communicate courageously. Your employees will understand and respect your courage and honesty. When you communicate openly and honestly, you are bound to make some mistakes but those mistakes will be better than the uninspiring communications.

9.Remember you are competing for attention. Every employee receives hundreds of communication every day. Your communication competes with all of them. Each person selects what to pay attention to and what to ignore. Ensure your piece of information stands out tall in the crowd and inspires them.

10.Important aspects should be kept important. The way the information is packaged and presented has a big impact on perceptions of the information and its content. And if you follow up your communication, it must be even more important. Too many executives think once they've communicated, they are done. There cannot be a bigger mistakes than this.

Communication is a holistic concept; everything we do conveys something about ourselves. If you want to achieve greatness in your chosen objectives you must communicate holistically. It is not enough to write well or to know a lot of big words. You must be able to project an image that will lead to success. You can change the way you appear to others by changing your behaviour pattern. If you want to change your behaviour pattern, you must change everything about yourself.

Great communicators practice a lot. Writers write and rewrite. Great orators like Winston Churchill and more contemporary speakers like Malcolm Gladwell practice and rehearse. They are good at what they do because they work at it.

> All successful endeavours are the result of good Interpersonal Communications

Barriers to Communication

Anything that prevents understanding of the message is a barrier to communication. These barriers can be thought of as filters, that is, the message leaves the sender, goes through these filters, and is then heard by the receiver. These filters may muffle the message.

1. Culture, background, and bias — You allow your past experiences to change the meaning of the message. Your culture, background, and bias are your hindering factors in understanding as to what others communicate to you.

2. Noise — Equipment or environmental noise impedes clear communication. The sender and the receiver must both be able to concentrate on the messages being sent to each other.

3. Yourself — Focusing on yourselves, rather than the other person can lead to confusion and conflict. Some of the factors that cause this type of confusions are defensiveness, superiority and ego.

> Nothing is so simple that it cannot be misunderstood.

4. Perception — Your preconceived attitudes affect your ability to listen. You listen uncritically to persons whom you like and dismiss those persons view with low status.

5. Message — Distractions happen when you focus on the facts rather than the idea. Semantic distractions occur when a word is used differently than you prefer. For example, the word foundress instead of founder, may cause you to focus on the word and not the message.

6. Environmental — Bright lights, an attractive person, unusual sights, or any other stimulus provides a potential distraction.

7. Smothering — Sometimes you take it for granted that things are understood on their own and you need not to take special effort to make them understand.

8. Stress — People do not see things the same way when under stress. What you see and believe at a given moment is influenced by your psychological frames of references — our beliefs, values, knowledge, experiences, and goals.

And the way to overcome filters is through active listening and feedback.

> One learns peoples through the heart, not the eyes or the intellect.
> Mark Twain

Active Listening

Hearing and listening are not one and the same. Hearing is the act of perceiving sound. It is involuntary and simply refers to the reception of aural stimuli.

Listening is a selective activity which involves the reception and the interpretation. It involves decoding the sound into meaning. Listening is divided into two main categories: passive and active. Active listening is listening with a purpose, reception and interpretation. Passive listening is little more than hearing. It occurs when the receiver of the message has little motivation to listen carefully.

People speak at 100 to 175 words per minute (WPM), but they can listen intelligently at 600 to 800 WPM. Since only a part of our mind is paying attention, it is easy to go into mind drift — thinking about other things while listening to someone. The cure for this is active listening — which involves listening with a purpose.

> The void created by the failure to communicate is soon filled with poison, drivel and misrepresentation.
> – C. Northcote

Active listening may be useful to gain information, obtain directions, understand others, solve problems, share interest, see how another person feels, show support, etc. It requires that the listener attends to the words and the feelings of the sender for understanding.

Listening requires more energy than speaking. It requires the receiver to hear the various messages, understand the meaning, and then verify the meaning by offering feedback. The following are some tips to improve your listening skills.

- Be aware of biases.
- Do not answer questions with questions.
- Do not become preoccupied with your own thoughts when others talk.
- Do not finish the sentences of others.
- Keep conversations on what others say, not on what interests them.
- Let the other speakers talk. Do not dominate the conversations.
- Never daydreams
- Plan responses after the others have finished speaking, not when they are speaking.
- Provide feedback, but do not interrupt incessantly.
- Spend more time listening than talking.
- Take brief notes. This forces you to concentrate on what is being said.

> Listening is not waiting for your chance to speak.

Feedback

Feedback, like listening , helps in reducing drawback in communication. The purpose of feedback is to alter messages so that intention of the original communicator is understood by the next communicator. Providing feedback is carried by paraphrasing the words of the sender. Restate the sender's feelings or ideas in your own words, rather than repeating their words. Nodding your head or dipping your eyebrows shows you don't quite understand the meaning of their phrase, or sucking air in deeply and blowing it hard shows that you are also exasperated with the situation.

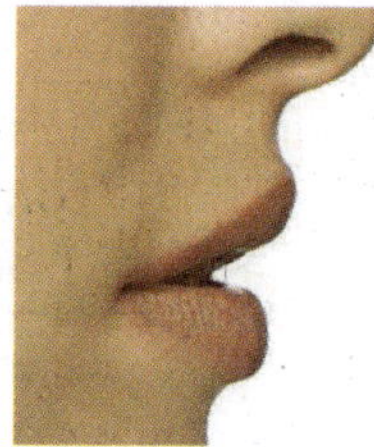

Carl Rogers listed five main categories of feedback. They are listed in the order in which they occur most frequently in daily conversations.

> Only the deaf and dumb will envy at people who speak much.
>
> Khalil Gibran

- **Evaluative**: Making a judgment about the worth, goodness, or appropriateness of the other person's statement.
- **Interpretive:** Paraphrasing — attempting to explain what the other person's statement means.
- **Supportive:** Attempting to assist or bolster the other communicator.
- **Probing:** Attempting to gain additional information, continue the discussion, or clarify a point.
- **Understanding:** Attempting to discover completely what the other communicator means by her statements.

> The important aspect of communication is not what is said but what is not said

Nonverbal Behaviour of Communication

To deliver the full impact of a message, use non-verbal behaviours to raise the level of interpersonal communication:

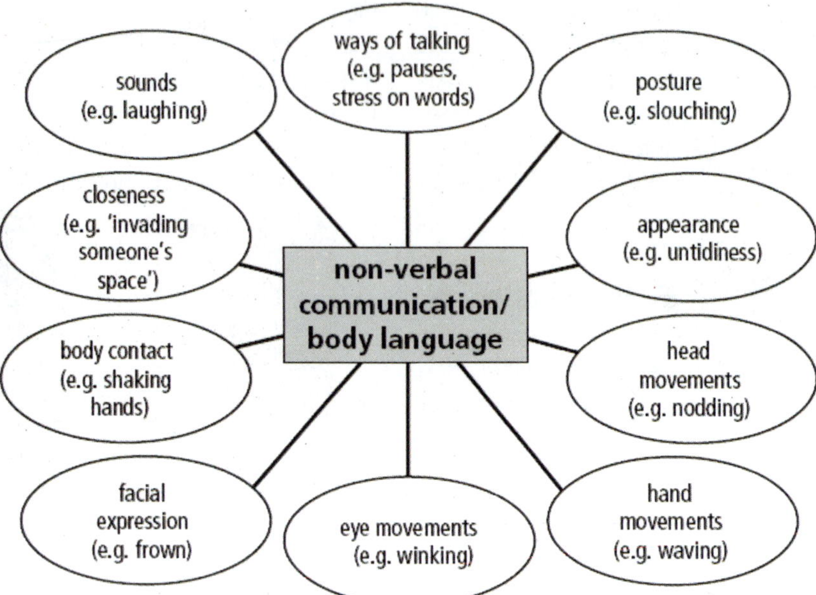

- **Eye contact:** This helps to regulate the flow of communication. It signals interest in others and increases the speaker's credibility. Good eye contact always opens the flow of communication and it also convey interest, concern, warmth, and credibility on the part of the communicator.
- **Facial Expressions:** Smiling is a powerful cue that transmits happiness, friendliness, warmth, and liking. So, if you smile frequently you will be perceived as more likable, friendly, warm and approachable. The listeners will be more comfortable around you and will want to listen more.
- **Gestures:** A lively speaking style will capture the listener's attention. It makes the conversation more interesting, and facilitates understanding. If you fail to gesture while speaking you may be perceived as boring and stiff.
- **Posture and body orientation:** Standing erect and leaning forward communicates to listeners that you are approachable, receptive and friendly. Interpersonal closeness results when you and the listener face each other. Speaking with your back turned or looking at the floor or ceiling communicates disinterest and should be avoided.
- **Proximity:** The distance you maintain while communicating with others depends on the cultural norms. It varies from culture to culture and place to place. Look for signals of discomfort and act accordingly.
- **Vocal:** vocal elements such as tone, pitch, rhythm, timbre, loudness, and inflection send a lot of communication signals. Try to adopt variations the above said elements. Speakers with monotone voice are perceived by listeners as boring and dull.

> The less people know, the more they yell. Seth Godin

Speaking Hints

- Be clear about what you say.
- Do not be vague, but on the other hand, do not complicate what you are saying with too much detail.
- Do not ignore signs of confusion.

- Ensure the receiver has a chance to comment or ask questions.
- Look at the receiver.
- Make sure your words match your tone and body language
- Speak comfortable words
- Try to put yourself in the other person's shoes
- Vary your tone and pace.
- When speaking ask the listeners if they are following you.

> Effective leadership is still largely a matter of communication.
>
> Alan Axelrod. Elizabeth I, CEO

Communication mistakes

Following are the mistakes the leaders bound to make while communicating with their bosses, colleagues and subordinates. They

- Don't recognize the importance of feedback.
- Fail to communicate their vision
- Fail to hold direct reports accountable for their behaviour.
- Fail to listen actively on a content level.
- Fail to recognize their level of influence.
- Fail to use feedback to improve.
- Spend 90% of energy.
- Think 'they' can change the person

> Regardles of the changes in technology, the market for well-crafted messages will always have an audience
>
> – Steve Burnett

Leadership Communication for Effective Teams

Effective teamwork is critical for organizational success, and the key to effective teams is effective communication. The quality of communication defines the effectiveness of a team.

Communicating effectively to the team

Level the Playing Field

There will always be differences in position, which can act as barriers in communication. Try to apply the concept of the round table to your team. You can remove the barrier by sitting along with your team members and communicating to them informally.

Take the Time

Communications has two essential parts, sending and receiving. Just because you send information does not mean it will be received as intended. The best way to check is to listen.

Remember that communication, by definition, is two-way.

Communicate Often and Appropriately

Unfortunately, there is no short cut to good communications and you need to take the time to do it well and be sensitive to the needs of others.

> The basic building block of good communications is the feeling that every human being is unique and of value. Unknown

Causes of poor leadership communication

Poor leadership communications can cripple even the most skilled teams. Poor communication has a negative impact on trust, productivity, and morale. There are three key reasons that contribute to communication problems in a team.

1.Power Imbalance

Power imbalances make open and honest conversation difficult, and it takes courage for an employee to tell the boss that he is wrong. Even though you treat your subordinates as equals, they never forget that you are the boss and you have power over them.

2.Expediency

You always run in short of time and there is never a plenty of time to do everything we ought to do. As result you fail to communicate everything to everybody. You also assume that people will come know things on their own and messages will be passed on. Failing to communicate consistently to all team members can create commotion in teams.

3.Lack of Detail

You often forget that your style of communication is the best possible in the world and you try to strike a difference from the others. But what you have to understand is that people may not see the big picture as you see it for yourself. Any idea that you present to the people should contain required information, otherwise it may frustrate the people however big your idea may be.

> The day soldiers stop bring you their problems is the day you have stopped leading them.
> – General Colin Powell

Critical component for an effective team communication is open, honest and effective two-way communications. Find ways to level the playing field and encourage dialogue. Take the time to adjust your messages to the individual and the circumstances.

Principles of communication for having an effective team

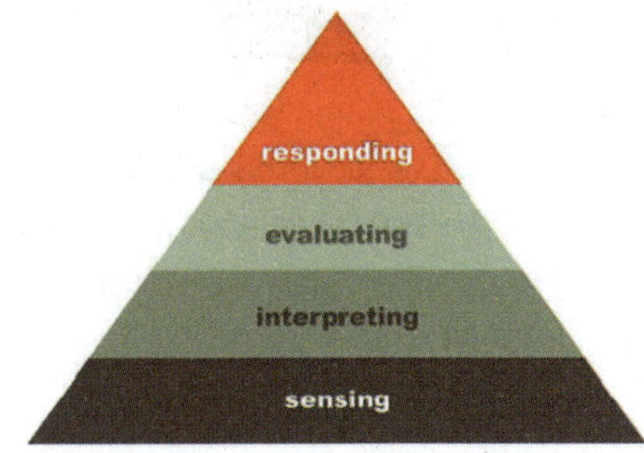

If you are going to adopt the following principles you are likely to achieve your goals through the team you are entrusted.

1. Ask more questions

While communicating with others, ensure that you not only pass on information, but also pose questions. Questioning is the key to influencing others towards positive change.

2. Be specific

You should try to hit the nail at its head and never beat around the bush. This will help you and others. Try to quantify your data and present them in number or chart whenever it is possible. Explain your view points by referring to concrete examples rather than abstract.

> Communicate unto the other person that which you would want him to communicate unto you if your positions were reversed.
> Aaron Goldman

3. Use positive language

Try to remain positive while communicating with people. Affirmative language is about that which you do want, would like, and do believe in. Do not focus your mind on the troubles that you faced or will be facing for continually thinking about what you do not want is not good.

4. Objective thinking

Develop your thinking by perceiving the facts without any distortion or prejudice. Learn to differentiate facts from fantasies. As a leader, you should think objectively and help others to have the same.

5. Focus on the future not the past

The past is gone. It cannot be changed. The future is not yet here. It can be changed. Therefore the focus of your communication should be based on the future, not the past. Your task is to help people to make decisions today that will shape a better tomorrow.

6.Identify Long term vs short term consequence

Prudent decisions are always taken keeping in mind the long term interest of the organisations. Let all your communication be focussed on long term benefits and not on the short-term pay off. The job of a leader is to change the mental focus of himself and his subordinates from the short-term effects to the long-term consequences.

7. Protect the self image

People with a good self-image are usually more productive. So to get the most out of people, always work to build up their self-image because people tend to act in accordance with their self-image.

Books for further reading

- Leadership communication, Deborah Barrett, McGraw-Hill Irwin, 2011.
- Leadership: a communication perspective, Michael Z. Hackman, Craig E. Johnson, Waveland Press, 1991.
- Effective leadership communication: a guide for department chairs and deans for managing difficult situations and people, Mary Lou Higgerson, Teddi A. Joyce, Anker Pub., 09-Jan-2007.
- The Leader As Communicator: Strategies and Tactics to Build Loyalty, Focus Effort, and Spark Creativity, Robert P. Mai, Alan Akerson, AMACOM Div American Mgmt Assn, 25-Apr-2003.
- Great Communication Secrets of Great Leaders, John Baldoni, McGraw-Hill; June 16, 2003.
- Leading Out Loud: Inspiring Change through Authentic Communications, New and Revised, Terry Pearce, Jossey-Bass; March 17, 2003.

- Management Communication: Principles and Practice, Michael Hattersley , Linda McJannet , McGraw-Hill/Irwin; January 19, 2007.
- Leadership communication, Ernest L. Stech, Nelson-Hall, 1983.
- The Language of Leaders: How Top CEOs Communicate to Inspire, Influence and Achieve Results, Kevin Murray, Kogan Page Publishers, 03-Nov-2011.
- Leadership: a communication perspective, Michael Z. Hackman, Craig E. Johnson, Waveland Press, 1991.
- Communication: The Key to Effective Leadership, Judith A. Pauley, Joseph F. Pauley, ASQ Quality Press, 03-Mar-2009.
- The Voice Of Authority, Booher, Tata McGraw-Hill Education, 01-Aug-2007.

14 Developing Human Network

LEARNING OUTCOME

- Introduction
- The meaning
- Networking is nothing but Relationship-Building
- Hidden Job Market- the factor compelling the growth of Networking
- Benefits of Networking
- Guidelines for Establishing and Maintaining a Successful Network
- Different networking approaches
- How to be successful in networking?
- Making networking work for you- Effective Networking
- Things you should never do
- The most popular social media networking or human networking sites are
- Books for further reading

> a good friend is a connection to life- a tie to the past, a road to the future, the key to sanity in a totally insane world

Introduction

Networking is essential no matter what business or position you are in. We are living in a new world filled with uncertainties. There is no such thing as job security since the world is experiencing corporate downsizing and self-employed workers are increasing day. Networking is the most important skill you will need to learn, develop and implement in order to get ahead and survive these uncertain times.

The meaning

Networking is the process of intentionally meeting people, making contacts, and forming relationships in hopes of gaining benefits such as career advice, job leads, business referrals, useful business information and ideas, and emotional support.

The human network is generally regarded as a social structure composed of individuals, business partners, friends or other organizations connected through technology, using devices such as personal computers, internets, cell phones, social networking websites and digital TVs.

Networking provides benefits pertaining to both social and business functions. It is mutually beneficial for their members. The relationships formed in networking help people create a larger world for themselves, with a variety of new relationships, opportunities, and resources.

Simply put, networking is relationship-building. Networking means developing and maintaining contacts and personal connections with a variety of people who might be helpful to you in your job search, career development and personal growth.

> When we get too caught up in the busyness of the world, we lose connection with one another - and ourselves

Networking is nothing but Relationship-Building

Networking is the art of building relationship. It is a critical skill for employees at all levels and in all job roles. It is often said that It Is Not What You Know, But WHO You Know. This maxim may not be completely true as there are other deciding factors like skills and knowledge which are also critical for job success. Still there is an element of truth in it because most positions are filled through referrals from employees' networks.

Lot of people believe that they do not have the personality or the skills to develop networking. Just view networking as getting to know others and letting others know you. You do not need to possess any extraordinary qualities to develop networking.

In order to develop networking, you need to have the following basic qualities.

1. Intrapersonal Development

The first relationship to consider is your relationship with yourself. Self awareness guides our personal development, helping us bring our best, authentic self to every interaction. Keep answering to questions like who am I? What are my strength and weakness, what do I value, what are my competencies? You need to do a kind of SWOT analysis.

2. Interpersonal Relationships

The quality of your interactions decides the trust and the connectivity. The quality of a relationship is determined by each interaction. It is important to understand interpersonal dynamics since it is your networking that will determine your success in the job market.

3. Group Dynamics and Culture

You are known by the company you keep is the maxim. The kind of people you move with and interact will decide your success. Ensure that you and your members contribute to the group in the expected lines. It is the collective environment that will pave way for innovation.

4. Collective Intelligence

What cannot be done on your own can be done by a group. When the many become one the result is multiplied. The collective intelligence always yields the expected result.

> A hidden connection is stronger than an obvious one.

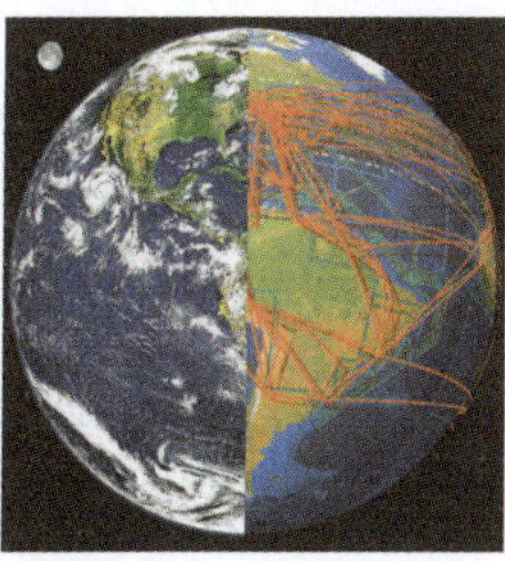

A survey says that 80% of the jobs are hidden, that is they are not advertised. The hidden job market exists because employers don't need to post every position that becomes vacant. They prefer to fill these positions in a cost effective and efficient way that is through networking.

In order to find out about non-advertised jobs you need to build your network. Networking helps you to establish new and future connections which will be advantageous to your current job search as well as your career. Talk to as many people as possible. You need to spend 80% of your search time on networking because 80% of the job is filled up by networking only.

Benefits of Networking

Frank K. Sonnenberg identified three main benefits of effective networking. They are referrals, relationships, and leads.

Referrals is very important particularly for growing a small business. Referrals take many forms e.g. a satisfied client might suggest others who may need the company's products or services, a network member who is familiar with the company's offerings might provide an endorsement, a network member may allow the small business owner to mention his or her name in marketing efforts and so on.

Establishing relationships is another benefit of networking which has a numerous positive outcomes. Forming a close relationship will provide invaluable insight into their needs. The insights gained from one relationship can often be applied to other person in order to improve those relationships. Close relationships can also provide information about competitors, their relative strengths and weaknesses, and what it takes to stay ahead of them.

> Our life is composed greatly from dreams, from the unconscious, and they must be brought into connection with action. They must be woven together.

Leads is another benefit of networking. It is useful particularly in new business opportunities, new career options and further networking possibilities. For example, the head of a construction company gives a lead of interior designer, and he in turn gives lead of furniture dealers and so on. In short, the benefits of networking can be listed as

- Developing other market contacts who may have more information
- Discovering job leads or opportunities that exist in your field
- Gaining advice on approaches to job searching, excelling at interviews
- Learning career and industry information, job market trends, growth areas
- Providing feedback on your résumé and cover letter

> Over 10 years ago, Human Resources and Skills Development Canada reported that 60% of all job openings were NOT listed or advertised. Today, it is estimated that more than 80% of job openings are never advertised to the general public and, instead, are filled through referrals from employees, moves and promotions within an organization, formal and informal networks, and job seekers who have contacted a company directly. In other words, more than 80% of today's jobs are filled through some form of networking.

Guidelines for Establishing and Maintaining a Successful Network

Who is my entire network?

Your network is all around you. They are faculty members, classmates, teaching assistants, family members, friends, acquaintances, employers and contacts from your home town. Let people know that you are actively job searching. Let them also know what you are looking for. Do not go about saying people that you just want a job. Instead make people understand what you are looking for so that they remember you and help you the best.

How do I network?

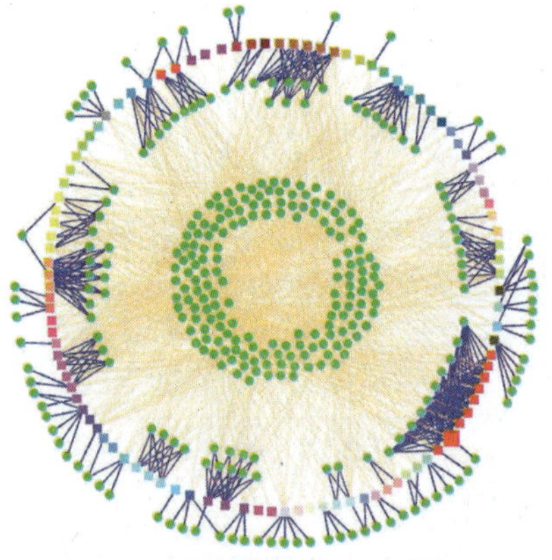

> The human connection--is the key to personal and career success.

Irrespective of what you are looking for, there are some basic steps that you should keep in mind in networking.

- create a contact list
- organise a contact list according to how people can help you
- create an advertisement/brochure of your skills and accomplishments
- make contact with those on your contact list

Different networking approaches

Talk to different people and make your availability and requirement known by informing them specifically the kind of jobs you are looking for. Get details of those who can be of use to you. Similarly ask your group members to contact you for any help.

Phone a prospective employer and introduce yourself and find out if there is opening. Write an email that introduces yourself and explains what you are looking for.

Look for volunteering opportunities in programmes conducted by clubs like Rotary, Lion, Leo, or NGOs. These are the places where you can exhibit talents and win the confidence of the potentials employers.

How to be successful in networking?

- Write down key information from contacts including names, phone numbers, fax numbers, email addresses, dates of communication, plus any pertinent information they share with you.
- Maintain an organized collection of business/networking cards to facilitate future contact with your network.
- Always keep your information up-to-date and maintain contact with your network.

Further develop your networking skills by attending different networking opportunities arranged by The Student Success Centre including: information sessions, career fairs, Students 2 Business Networking event, Business after Five, and many others.

> Our big goal should be to make connection to the Internet as common as connection to telephones is today.

Making networking work for you- Effective Networking

If you are going to take time and attend networking events, try to get the most out of them. Many people attend these events and do nothing to network. They are often seen just sitting in the corner and watch. But by just observing the event you will never get anything out of it. Networking doesn't work for you as long as you don't work at it.

The ability to do effective networking is an often overlooked leadership skill, but it's one that will greatly assist you in getting the career you want. Networking is simultaneously one of the most self-evident and dreaded challenges that aspiring leaders must address. Effective networking requires getting out there and connecting with others, no matter how uncomfortable it feels. Here are some ways in which you can improve your networking skills.

1. Practice Positive Networking

Positive networking will take the stress out of networking. doing a task with a positive note will always reduce the pain involved in it. It is always tough to find what the other person wants and is interested in. it requires a natural conversation starter to initiate the discussion.

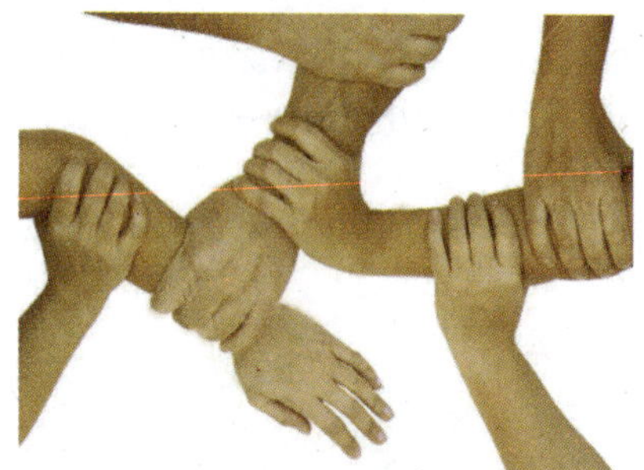

2. Hand out Business Cards

Ensure that you always carry your business card. The easiest step to improve your networking skills is to stash your business cards everywhere—in the pockets of all your pants and shirts, in your bag, in your car and so on.

3. Make Others Feel More Comfortable

It's important to remember that 80 per cent of people are uncomfortable in networking situations. Adopt a host mentality and try to include everyone in the conversation.

4. Just Say Yes!

When you receive an invitation to an event, instead of making excuses try to find ways and means to be there. You never know something amazing might happen.

> All human beings are interconnected, one with all other elements in creation. Henry Reed

5. Contribute More than Your Presence

Mere presence is not going to help you. Your success depends on your contribution to the event. Stay positive and make your presence felt in an appreciable manner.

6. A Cure for Networking Nervosus

In case you are worried about making it alone to the events, take a teammate. It beats going solo and you can be on each other's backup. A teammate can be a client, friend, colleague or a potential business associate.

7. Follow up Fast and Be Brief

If you promise to do something, do it right away. Everyone is busy so send short emails. In networking reliability builds your good reputation. Return phone calls or emails the following day. If you are sending an article or information that is more than a couple of paragraphs, highlight the key information.

8. Be a Connector

The true sign of a networker is being a connector. At social and business events make it a habit of introducing people to one and other if you see that they might have mutual interests or could help each other. But connecting doesn't stop when the networking event ends. In fact do it as a matter of habit.

The bonus of becoming more engaged and building a network is personal happiness and well being. Research shows that people who are more connected are healthier and have a greater sense of well being and happiness. So, don't do it just for career advancement; do it for your life!

> Only through our connectedness to others can we really know and enhance the self.
> Harriet Goldhor Lerner

In short here are some ways to make the most out of networking events

1. Introduce yourself to at least five people at each event.
2. Don't do all the talking. Ask questions, take the time to get to know others and learn about their business. People love to talk and you can learn a lot by listening.
3. Keep smiling. This may look simple but it is important. Just smile and others will notice you.
4. Exchange business cards with people you want to follow up with.
5. Ask people you meet what other networking events they attend and which ones they find most beneficial.
6. Have fun and relax yourself at events of this kind

Things you should never do

1. Provide only relevant information

Remember, social networking is about connecting with people. Therefore, make sure you add a few details about your life, your hobbies, your preferences, etc. Do you have kids? Dogs? Like to travel? Read? Whatever it is, make sure you put it on your profile. The information you provide should make sure your personality comes through. Don't just list a dry and boring description that could be mentioned on a resume. Let people know who you are.

2. Never share too many personal data

If you wouldn't be comfortable sharing this at a networking event, then you probably shouldn't be sharing it on your social networking profile. What types of details about your life would you feel comfortable telling? Those are good ones to share on your profile. Leave off those types of things would you not want your client to know about.

3.Don't do too much selling.

Selling too much on your profile or in your social networking activities is much the same thing as thrusting your business cards, ,trying to handover brochures and sales letters to as many people as possible in a meeting. Remember, the idea behind social networking is building relationships and not annoying people.

> For men and women, the language of conversation is primarily a language of establishing connections and negotiating relationships.
>
> Deborah Tannen

The most popular social media networking or human networking sites are

1. Twitter: www.twitter.com—This has become a favourite because of its ease of use. It's great for making connections you wouldn't otherwise be able to make, and for quick sharing of information.
2. Linked in: www.linkedin.com—Offers a great search function and a way to connect with others in a group,

ask questions and learn more about someone professionally.

3. Facebook: www.facebook.com—The #1 social network in terms of users, surpassing MySpace in April, 2008. For that reason alone, you should at least check it out. Businesses have become listed on Facebook with their pages, and you can become a "fan" or a "member", depending on their angle.
4. Ning network: www.ning.com—There are thousands of Ning networks out there, and chances are you've visited them without even knowing it, because many networks have paid to use their own domain name instead of including "ning" at the end. These networks allow you to connect for free or as members on a specific subject or with a specific group of people with similar interests.
5. Blogs–yours or others. You can showcase your expertise through your own posts or at others" blogs

Books for further reading

- Social Networking for Business: Choosing the Right Tools and Resources to fit your needs, Rawn Shah, Pearson Prentice Hall, 2010.
- Sensing and Modelling Human Networks, Tanzeem Khalid Choudhury, Massachusetts Institute of Technology, 2004.
- Helping ourselves: families and the human network, Mary C. Howell, Beacon Press, 1975.
- Natural helping networks: a strategy for prevention, Alice H. Collins, Diane L. Pancoast, National Association of Social Workers, 1976.
- The Ecology of Human Development: Experiments by Nature and Design, Urie Bronfenbrenner, Harvard University Press, 1979.
- The Evolving Human and the Future World, Pawan Raina, M.D. Publications Pvt. Ltd., 2006.
- Computational Social Network Analysis: Trends, Tools and Research Advances, Ajith Abraham et al, Springer, 21-Dec-2009.
- Social Network Analysis: A Handbook, John Scott, SAGE, 25-Mar-2000.
- Social Network Analysis: Methods and Applications, Stanley Wasserman, Katherine Faust, Cambridge University Press, 25-Nov-1994.
- Network analysis: studies in human interaction, Jeremy Boissevain, James Clyde Mitchell, Mouton, 1973.
- Fifth Generation Management: Integrating Enterprises Through Human Networking, Charles M. Savage, Digital Press; 1 edition (March 14, 1990)
- The Connect Effect: Building Strong Personal, Professional, and Virtual Networks, Michael Dulworth, Berrett-Koehler Publishers (January 1, 2008).
- The Networking Book: People Connecting with People, Jessica Lipnack, Jeffrey Stamps, Routledege Publication, 1986

15 Balancing Work and Life

LEARNING OUTCOME

- Meaning
- What Work-Life Balance Is Not.
- Importance of Work-Life Imbalance
- Gender differences regarding work-life balance
- Work-life balance issues and their influence on children
- Work life balance & the responsibility of the employer
- Tips for balancing work and life
- Tips For Tough Times
- Is Work-Personal Life Balance Achievable?
- Elements of an Acceptable Work-Life Compromise
- Steven Covey's way of WORK LIFE BALANCE
- Books for further reading

> Life is like riding a bicycle. To keep your balance you must keep moving.
> – Albert Einstein

The expression was first used in the late 1970s to describe the balance between an individual's work and personal life. In the United States, this phrase was first used in 1986.

The topic has gained more importance today than in the past, because, in the past, people often were attending to one major role in their life that is the male were going for jobs and female were looking after the children. But today, the employees play a dual role of going for a job and looking after the family. This is very much applicable particularly to working women.

Many employees all over the world are experiencing burnout due to over work. This condition is seen in nearly all occupations from blue collar workers to upper management. Experts say that there are many causes for this situation ranging from personal ambition and the pressure of family obligations to the accelerating pace of technology. According to a recent study for the Center for Work-Life Policy, 1.7 million people consider their jobs and their work hours excessive because of globalization.

Loyalty and a sense of corporate community have been replaced by a work culture that expects more and more from their employees yet offers little security in return. In fact the past 30 years have experienced an increase in work due to intense competitive work environment.

Meaning

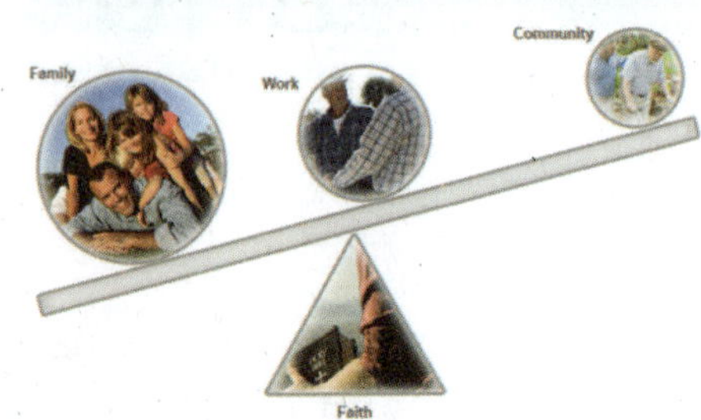

> Nature does not hurry, yet everything is accomplished.
> – Lao Tzu

Work–life balance is prioritizing between work on the one hand and life on the other. Work refers to career and ambition and life refers to health, pleasure, leisure, family and spiritual development.

That is, work refers to achievement and life refers to enjoyment.

The term work-life balance applies to a person's effort to be effective in their work life and as well as in their personal life. You must learn to balance your professional goals with your personal responsibilities. They –the personal and professional goals must live in harmony together. Otherwise, you end up resentful, become unhappy in life and lose sense of what is truly important.

> When people go to work, they shouldn't have to leave their hearts at home. Betty Bender

What Work-Life Balance Is Not.

1. Work-Life Balance does not mean an equal balance. It is not possible to schedule equal number of hours for both work and life. It is going to be unrealistic exercise. We should have a flexi schedule to fit into the daily routine.

2. Work-Life Balance does not mean have a fixed schedule. Work-life balance will vary from time to time, stage to stage of life. The schedule that you have for today may not work for you for your tomorrow. Similarly your work-life balance depends on the stage of life in which you are living in e.g. it is different when you are unmarried and married, stay with the spouse and stay away from the spouse, having children and not having children, new career and nearing retirement.

3. Work-Life Balance does not mean one-size fits all, balance. There cannot be one work-life balance that may fit all. All of us are unique and therefore the best work-life balance is different for each of us. After all we all have different priorities and different lives.

> One machine can do the work of fifty ordinary men. No machine can do the work of one extraordinary man.
>
> – Elbert Hubbard

Importance of Work-Life Imbalance

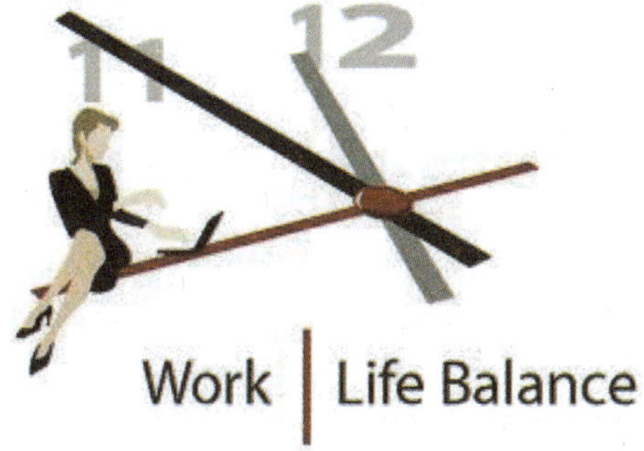

Brian G. Dyson, former Coca-Cola Enterprises president and CEO, once said, "Imagine life as a game in which you are juggling some five balls in the air. You name them—work, family, health, friends, and spirit—and you're keeping all of these in the air. You will soon understand that work is a rubber ball. If you drop it, it will bounce back. But the other four balls—family, health, friends, and spirit— are made of glass. If you drop one of these, they will be irrevocably scuffed, marked, nicked, damaged, or even shattered. They will never be the same. You must understand that and strive for balance in your life."

According to a survey conducted by the National Life Insurance Company, four out of ten employees state that their jobs are "very" or "extremely" stressful. Those in high stress jobs are three times more likely than others to suffer from stress-related medical conditions and are twice as likely to quit. The study states that women, in particular, report stress related to the conflict between work and family.

> Women need real moments of solitude and self-reflection to balance out how much of ourselves we give away."
>
> –Barbara de

Gender differences regarding work-life balance

According to Sylvia Hewlett, president of the Centre for Work-Life Policy, if a woman takes time off to care for children or an older parent, employers tend to see these people as less than fully committed. It's as though their identity is transformed.

Brett Graff, Nightly Business Report correspondent states that a woman may have trouble re-entering the market or, if she does find a position, it will likely be a lower position with less pay. Most will want to re-enter, by accepting lesser positions or lower wages. This circumstance only increases the work-life balance stress experienced by many women employees.

> One of the symptoms of an approaching nervous breakdown is the belief that one's work is terribly important.
> –Bertrand Russell

Work-life balance issues and their influence on children

The children are today raised by maids or childcare centres. The children are more likely to come to an empty house and spend time with Video games, Television and Internet.

No one knows how many kids are home after school without an adult at home. The number is expected to be in the millions. Also, according to a study by the National Institute of Child Health and Human Development, the more time that children spent in child care, the more likely their teachers were to report problem behaviour of the children.

> The more I want to get something done, the less I call it work.
> – Richard Bach

Work life balance & the responsibility of the employer

The employers have begun to realise that work life balance have direct impact on productivity. Research shows that those employees who have favourable work-life balance have a greater pride in their organization.

> Being busy does not always mean real work.
> – Thomas A. Edison

To ensure work-life balance employers can offer flexible working arrangements, casual and telecommuting work, compulsory leave, strict maximum hours and foster an environment that encourages employees not to continue to work after working hours.

Ask yourself now, when was the last time you achieved and enjoyed something at work? What about achieved and enjoyed with your family; your friends? And how recently have you achieved and enjoyed something just for you?

Why not take 20 minutes on the way home from work and do something just for yourself? And when you get home, before you walk in the door, think about whether you want to focus on achieving or enjoying at home tonight. Then act accordingly when you do walk in the door.

> To find joy in work is to discover the fountain of youth.
> – Pearl S. Buck

At work you can create your own best work-life balance by making sure you not only achieve, but also reflect the joy of the job, and the joy of life, every day. If nobody pats you on the back today, pat yourself on the back. And help others to do the same.

When you do, when you are a person that not only gets things done, but also enjoys the doing, it attracts people to you. They want you on their team and they want to be on your team.In order to maintain the delicate balance between work and life, try the following:

Tips for balancing work and life

1.Focus. When you're at work, focus on work and when you're at home, focus on home. Clear your mind of nagging obligations.

2.Keep your tables clean. Keep your tables at home and at the office clean. An untidy table leads to an untidy mind and hence you will not be able to focus.

3.Make lists. At the end of a workday make a list for the following day. Listing the events helps you release the tension both at home and at the office.

> When your work speaks for itself, don't interrupt.
> – Henry J. Kaiser

4.Focus on the Important. Before beginning to work on the listed items, arrange them in order of importance. Work on the highest-priority items first.

5. Don't procrastinate. Postponing the work until the last minute not only develops stress in you, but also results in wasting time worrying about the work, rather than taking productive steps to complete it.

6. Don't be a slave to your e-mail/ mobile phone calls. Try to avoid having e-mail and phone calls interrupt your work unless it is going to be essential in your execution. You should try to manage the day instead of the day managing you. You should aim to maximise your productivity and never allow the unfinished tasks to eat up your persona time.

7. Improve your skills to enhance your productivity. Get the help of experts in case you have to depend largely on computers or on line activities. Where possible go for a crash course to familiarise yourself with those modern gadgets.

8. Set Your Own Standards. Establish your own principles of operations. Define the few principles by which you will operate your business and your life. Let them guide you instead of following what the others follow or what the society likes.

> Never work just for money or for power. They won't save your soul or help you sleep at night.
> – Marian Wright Edelman

9. Delegate. Certain tasks can be performed better when outsourced than doing by yourself. Identify those tasks that can be outsource. Similarly delegate the assignments to people who have the ability to perform better than you.

10. Be flexible. It is a fast changing world. Only those who are flexible can be productive. You need to adjust yourself with the changes that take place around you.

11. Learn to say no. Being a good employee, spouse, parent, and friend doesn't mean yielding to everyone else's demands and spending all your time and energy doing for others. Think about the common and personal objectives, and find ways to achieve them.

12. Take time for yourself. Find time for yourself. Try to take 10 or 15 minutes from the routine to do things that you like. That will help you to enjoy life more and people around you will find you a more pleasant person.

13. Maintain Your Energy. You need lot of energy to remain productive and focussed. Sleep well and eat a balanced diet. Exercise at least 15 to 20 minutes a day.

> Take a break or else you will break.
> – Dr.K.Alex

14. Bury the guilt feelings. We are human beings and are bound to make mistakes. The mistakes that we have committed may make us to develop guilt feelings. Guilt feelings that leads to a positive change is useful. But guilt that turns out to be negative will prove to be useless and it keeps us stuck and prevents fro progressing.

15. Develop relationships, both at work and home. Form a good relationship both at home and at work. For that relationship will foster teamwork and create an environment in which people will respect you help you in whatever you do.

15. Don't Worry. Instead of worrying about things that had happened concentrate on resolving those things. Worrying is bad for your health and it reduces your energy level. Channel your energy into more productive uses.

16. Have some blank Space on Your Calendar. Never fill your calendar with programmes. Take a break. The best ideas have come only when the people were found relaxing. Find out some time for reflection. Albert Einstein, Sir Isaac Newton, Archimedes and many others were relaxing when they came up with their world-changing ideas.

> Never work just for money or for power. They won't save your soul or help you sleep at night.
> – Marian Wright Edelman

Tips For Tough Times

Experts say that when people are faced with lot of problems, they should indulge in self-talk. Practicing self-talk de-escalates stress and confidence is regained. Whenever you find yourself in a testing environment, read these statements to yourself.

> To say "too busy" is merely to say "confused priorities."
> – Jonathan Lockwood Huie

1. As long as I keep my cool, I am in control of myself.

2. I do not need to prove myself in any situation. I can stay calm.
3. I don't need to feel threatened. I can relax and stay cool.
4. I feel angry; that must mean I'm hurt or scared. My anger is a signal. Time to talk to myself and relax.
5. If people criticize me, I can survive that. Nothing says I have to be perfect.
6. If people want to go off the wall, that is their thing. I do not need to respond to their anger or feel threatened.
7. It is impossible to control other people and situations. The only thing I can control is myself and how I express my feelings.
8. It is nice to have other people's love and approval, but even without it, I can still accept and like MYSELF.
9. It is okay to be uncertain or insecure sometimes. I do not need to be in control of everything and everybody.
10. Most things we argue about are stupid and insignificant. My anger results from having old primary feelings restimulated. It is okay to walk away from this fight.
11. No need to doubt myself. What other people say doesn›t matter. I am the only person who can make me mad or keep me calm.
12. Nothing says I have to be competent and strong all the time. It is okay to feel unsure or confused.
13. People put erasers on the ends of pencils for a reason. It is okay to make mistakes.
14. People will act the way they want to, not the way I want them to.
15. Time to relax and slow things down. Take TIME OUT.
16. When I get into an argument, I can stay with my plan and know what to do. I can take a TIME OUT.

> Far and away the best prize that life offers is the chance to work hard at work worth doing.
>
> –Theodore Roosevelt

Is Work-Life Balance Achievable?

There is no such thing as a perfect work-personal life balance. Just as there's no such thing as a perfect balance because life is unpredictable and imperfect.

Elements of an Acceptable Work-Life Compromise

There are opposing forces pushing and pulling you in all directions. Whether it's balancing or compromising, what we want is living a satisfied life. In order to do this, there are three essential things we need to keep in front of us to balance our work and life.

Priorities

The first essential element involves taking a long, hard and realistic look at your priorities. Whether you work outside the home or have your own business, have kids or pets or aging parents, or have hobbies you need to be able to rank the importance of all aspects of your life.

It's important to recognize that your priorities will change, sometimes frequently, and if you're not clear on what parts of your life need your attention first, achieving an acceptable compromise will be a struggle.

Flexibility

Because your priorities will change, and life has a way of introducing unexpected and sometimes unwanted surprises, you need to be flexible in order to accommodate these changes, regroup and shuffle your priorities, and change directions when necessary. By avoiding looking at your priorities as set in stone, you'll gain the flexibility you need to move with the changes.

Acceptance

The reality is that some days are better than others and some priorities will be easier to satisfy than others. The key is to remember that with a constant give and take, you can trust that it will eventually all even out in the end.

The following actions can reduce your stress level in the workplace and in many other aspects of your life:

1. Acknowledge at the end of the day, each week, what you did that was good.
2. Build a support system of co-workers and friends.
3. Distinguish between what you can change and what you can't; accept the givens.
4. Establish a priority list of job tasks and learn to delegate.
5. Mix up stress and non-stress projects.
6. Provide your own reinforcements.
7. Recognize internal sources of stress.
8. Re-examine your values - clarify what is important in the roles you play.
9. Set limits.
10. Take things less personally.
11. View yourself as having alternatives and choices.

Steven Covey's way of WORK LIFE BALANCE

The Seven Habits of Highly Effective People author Steven R. Covey advises readers how to strike a balance between work and life:

Today the average college student or corporate worker considers themselves a "multitasker." It's not unusual to meet people in their 20s who are working, going to school, starting their own company, married, raising kids, and enjoying hobbies. They end up with a huge list of things that fracture their attention. This isn't wrong in any way—for the most part it's admirable—but there is an old saying: to a hammer, everything looks like a nail.

To a chronic multitasker, everything is a task. Soon, the things in life that are really important to them are in the same list as everything else, and the only tasks that get done are the ones that have become urgent, but often aren't very important.

Covey explains that striking your balance means not just responding to "the four P's"—those items that are Pressing, Proximate, Pleasant, or Popular—but by prioritizing the tasks that are important to you in the grand scheme. On most days, easier said than done. Thanks, Covey! a recent study of more than 50,000 employees from a variety of manufacturing and service organizations found that two out of every five employees are dissatisfied with the balance between their work and their personal lives. The lack of balance "is due to long work hours, changing demographics, more time in the car, the deterioration of boundaries between work and home, and increased work pressure," says the study's author, Bruce Katcher, president of the Discovery Group, a management consulting firm.

Books for further reading

- Balancing Work and Family, Jacqueline Wallen, Allyn & Bacon; December 28, 2001.
- Balancing Your Life: Executive Lessons for Work, Family and Self, James G. S. Clawson, World Scientific Publishing Company, July 30, 2009.
- Big Rocks: Balancing Life & Work, Gary F. Russell, Lifestyle Press, 01-Apr-2006.
- Balancing Work & Life, Robert Holden, Ben Renshaw, Dorling Kindersley Limited, 01-Jul-2009.
- A Balanced Life: Living the Hula Hoop Principle, Charles B. Beckert, Derry L. Brinley, Cedar Fort, 01-Dec-2006.
- The Balancing Act, Fiona Parashar, Simon & Schuster UK, 22-Feb-2005
- My Life and Work, Henry Ford, Cosimo Inc., 30-Nov-2007.
- On the fly guide to--balancing work and life, Bill Butterworth, Waterbrook Press, 18-Jul-2006.
- Balancing life and work: the humanities as an essential part of career exploration, Leslie Haynes et al, Northwest Regional Education Laboratory, 1998.
- From Work-Family Balance to Work-Family Interaction: Changing the Metaphor, Diane F. Halpern, Susan E. Murphy, Routledge, 2005.

16 Practising Corporate Social Responsibility (CSR)

LEARNING OUTCOME

- What does CSR mean?
- Other definitions
- Goal of CSR
- Areas of CSR
- Need For CSR:
- Benefits of CSR
- Argument in favour of CSR:
- Argument against CSR:
- Factors that promote CSR:
- Limiting factor in Implementing CSR:
- India and CSR
- CSR activities carried out by Companies in India
- List of projects for funding under CSR:
- How to implement CSR commitments
- Books for further reading

> Always do right; this will gratify some people and astonish the rest.
> – Mark Twain

What does CSR mean?

The term "corporate social responsibility" came in to common use in the late 1960s and early 1970s, after many multinational corporations formed.

Corporate social responsibility commonly known as CSR is a form of corporate self-regulation integrated into a business model. CSR is also called corporate conscience, corporate citizenship, social performance, or sustainable responsible business.

> Vision without action is a daydream. Action without vision is a nightmare.
> –Japanese Proverb

CSR is about how companies manage their business to produce an overall positive impact on society.

The term CSR generally applies to company efforts that go beyond what may be required by regulators.

CSR generally involves incurring expenses that do not provide an immediate financial benefit to the company, but instead promote positive social and environmental change. CSR may also be referred to as corporate citizenship.

Corporate Social Responsibility (CSR) is becoming an increasingly important activity to businesses nationally and internationally. As globalisation accelerates and large corporations serve as global providers, these corporations have progressively recognised the benefits of providing CSR programs in their various locations. CSR activities are now being undertaken throughout the globe.

> What is the use of a house if you haven't got a tolerable planet to put it on? Henry David

Lord Holme and Richard Watts, defines "Corporate Social Responsibility is the continuing commitment by business to behave ethically and contribute to economic development while improving the quality of life of the workforce and their families as well as of the local community and society at large"

Other definitions

Corporate social responsibility (CSR) is the process by which businesses negotiate their role in society.

MNCs generally define CSR as Triple P: People, Planet and Profit.

"CSR is about capacity building for sustainable livelihoods. It respects cultural differences and finds the business opportunities in building the skills of employees, the community and the government"

"CSR is about business giving back to society"

"Operating a business in a manner that meets or exceeds the ethical, legal, commercial and public expectations that society has of business" the European Commission defines "A concept whereby companies decide voluntarily to contribute to a better society and a cleaner environment.

> We have a responsibility to look after our planet. It is our only home.
> – Henry David

A concept whereby companies integrate social and environmental concerns in their business operations and in their interaction with their stakeholders on a voluntary basis".

Corporate Social Responsibility (CSR) is defined as the way companies integrate social, environmental, and economic concerns into their values and operations in a transparent and accountable manner.

Goal of CSR

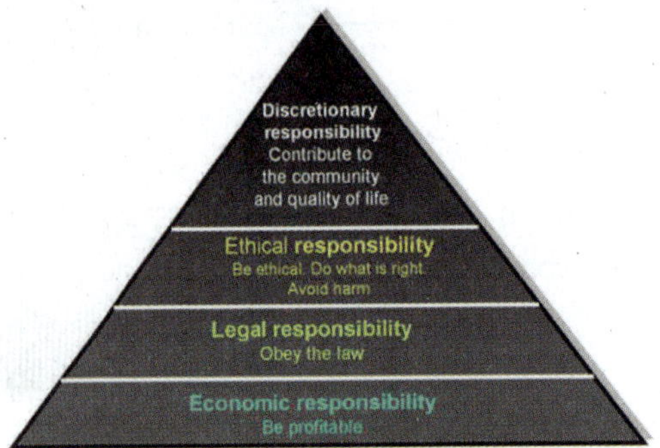

The goal of CSR is to embrace responsibility for the company's actions and encourage a positive impact through its activities on the environment, consumers, employees, communities, stakeholders and all other members of the public sphere. CSR is the deliberate inclusion of public interest into corporate decision-making.

The goal of CSR has been articulated in a number of ways. In essence it is about building sustainable businesses, which need healthy economies, markets and communities.

The key drivers for CSR are

1. **Enlightened self-interest** - creating a synergy of ethics, a cohesive society and a sustainable global economy where markets, labour and communities are able to function well together.

2. **Social investment** - contributing to physical infrastructure and social capital is increasingly seen as a necessary part of doing business.

> Since after extinction no one will be present to take responsibility, we have to take full responsibility now. Jonathan Schell

3. **Transparency and trust** - business has low ratings of trust in public perception.

There is increasing expectation that companies will be more open, more accountable and be prepared to report publicly on their performance in social and environmental arenas.

4. **Increased public expectations of business** - globally companies are expected to do more than merely provide jobs and contribute to the economy through taxes and employment."

> The future is not completely beyond our control. It is the work of our own hands.
> – Robert F. Kennedy

Areas of CSR

There are many areas of business operations that are affected by CSR. The most often mentioned areas of CSR are:

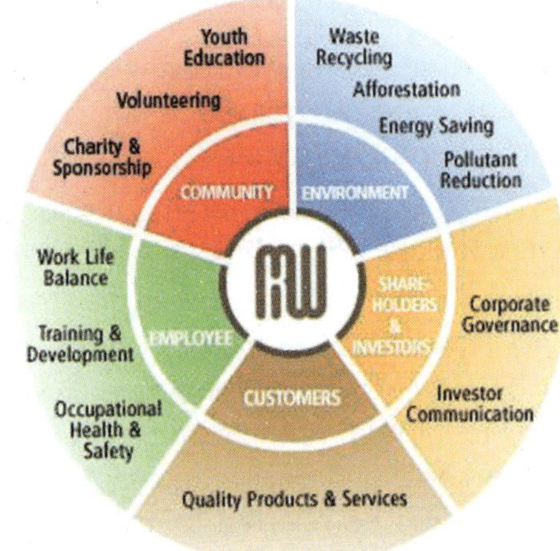

Governance: sound governance, ethical conduct of staff, transparency of operations, no conflicts of interest, compliance with listing rules, compliance with corporate law.

Risk Management: organizational health & safety, product safety, regulatory compliance, reputation management, responsible business practices, stakeholder engagement.

Value Chain: responsible procurement, supplier management, externalization of costs, supplier screening, supplier feedback, fair trade.

> Modern society will find no solution to the ecological problem unless it takes a serious look at its lifestyle.
> – Pope John Paul II

Social: human rights, community engagement, philanthropic activities, charitable donations, staff volunteering, social benefits, local capacity building, social investment

Employees: turnover, morale, satisfaction, work-life balance, internal culture (transparency), labour practices, job security, remuneration, diversity, equal opportunity, training

Environment: environmental footprint, waste & pollution avoidance, eco-efficiency, product recycling, sustainability, greenhouse gas emissions, resource reduction, precautionary principle

Measurement: GRI (Global Reporting Initiative) reporting, internal & external audits, verification statements, management targets.

> We can no longer have every thing we want but we can be more than we imagined
> – Howard Jerome

Need For CSR:

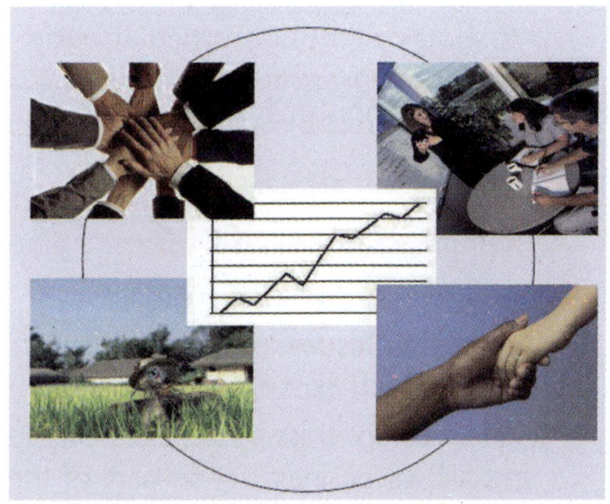

Ethics in business has been an issue for academics, practitioners and government regulators for decades , some believe that unethical, immoral and/ or illegal behaviour is widespread in the business world. Numerous scandals in the 20th century seemed to add credence to the criticism of business ethics.

1. The shrinking role of government

In the past, governments have relied on legislation and regulation to deliver social and environmental objectives in the business sector. Shrinking government resources, coupled with a distrust of regulations, has led to the exploration of voluntary and non-regulatory initiatives instead.

2. Demands for greater disclosure

There is a growing demand for corporate disclosure from stakeholders, including customers, suppliers, employees, communities, investors, and activist organizations.

3. Increased customer interest

There is evidence that the ethical conduct of companies exerts a growing influence on the purchasing decisions of customers. In a recent survey by *Environics International*, more than one in five consumers reported having either rewarded or punished companies based on their perceived social performance.

> The level of consumption that we identify with success is utterly unsustainable. We're gobbling up the world. John Robbins

4. Growing investor pressure

Investors are changing the way they assess companies' performance, and are making decisions based on criteria that include ethical concerns. The Social Investment Forum reports that in the US in 1999, there was more than $2 trillion worth of assets invested in portfolios that used screens linked to the environment and social responsibility. A separate survey by *Environics International* revealled that more than a quarter of share-owning Americans took into account ethical considerations when buying and selling stocks. (More on socially responsible investment can be found in the 'Banking and investment' section of the site.)

> The universe is a communion of subjects, not a collection of objects.
> – Thomas Berry

5. Competitive labour markets

Employees are increasingly looking beyond paychecks and benefits, and seeking out employers whose philosophies and operating practices match their own principles. In order to hire and retain skilled employees, companies are being forced to improve working conditions.

6. Supplier relations

As stakeholders are becoming increasingly interested in business affairs, many companies are taking steps to ensure that their partners conduct themselves in a socially responsible manner. Some are introducing codes of conduct for their suppliers, to ensure that other companies' policies or practices do not tarnish their reputation.

> Our lives begin to end the day we become silent about things that matter.
> – Martin Luther King, Jr.

Benefits of CSR

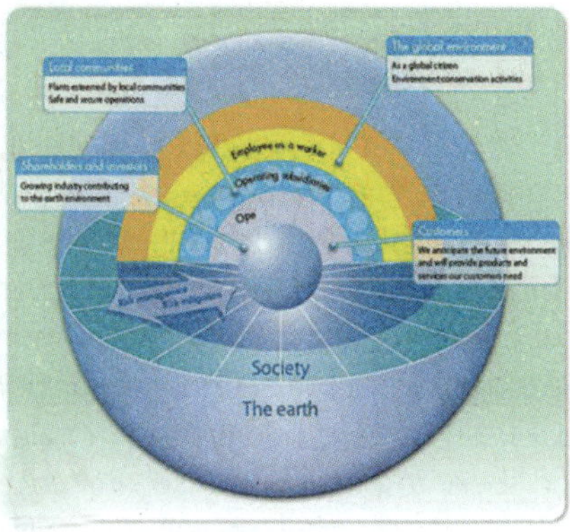

1. Benefits to the company

- Access to capital;
- Enhanced brand image and reputation;
- Greater productivity and quality;
- Improved financial performance;
- Increased sales and customer loyalty;
- Lower operating costs;
- More ability to attract and retain employees;
- Product safety and decreased liability.
- Reduced regulatory oversight;
- Workforce diversity;

2. Benefits to the society at large

- Charitable contributions;
- Corporate involvement in community education, employment and homelessness programmes;
- Employee volunteer programmes;
- Product safety and quality.

3. Environmental benefits:

- Better product durability and functionality;
- Greater material recyclability;
- Greater use of renewable resources;
- Integration of environmental management tools into business plans, including life-cycle assessment and costing, environmental management standards, and eco-labelling.

> We should all be concerned about the future because we have to spend the rest of our lives there.
> – Francis

Argument in favour of CSR:

- Addresses issues by being proactive
- Addresses issues by using business resources and expertise
- Addresses social issues business caused and allows business to be part of the solution
- CSR is in business's long-term self-interest

- Ethical Imperative
- Limits future government intervention
- Protects business self-interest

Argument against CSR:

- Business already has enough power
- Business is not equipped to handle social activities
- Cost of social action is passed on to consumers
- CSR decreases competitiveness (esp. international)
- Dilutes the primary aim of business
- Increase business power
- Limits the ability to compete in a global marketplace
- Management's only responsibility is to maximize the profits of its owners.
- Restricts the free market goal of profit maximization

> Never doubt that a small group of thoughtful, committed citizens can change the world. Indeed it is the only thing that ever has.
>
> – Margaret Mead

Factors that promote CSR:

- Advances in Communication
- Advocacy
- Competitive advantage
- Consumerism
- Ethical culture.
- Globalisation
- Governance
- Leadership
- Sustainable development

> All things are possible once enough human beings realize that everything is at stake.
>
> – Norman Cousins

Limiting factor in Implementing CSR:

- Country- and context-specific issues;
- Failure to integrate CSR initiatives into a larger development plan.
- Failure to involve the beneficiaries of CSR;
- Failure to see CSR as innovation
- Lack of human resources;
- Lack of vision
- Maintaining old structures
- Non-Participative Management.
- One world approaches
- Risk/ Opportunity roles.
- Scale of change
- Selective hearing
- Social attitudes of oil company staff and a focus on technical and managerial solutions;
- Sub- Strategic Management
- Uneven Approaches

> It's not where you are, it's where you're headed that matters.
>
> – Joey Smallwood

India and CSR

Indian companies have now come together to discharge their stakeholder wishes and societal obligations, along with the wealth maximisation goal. Nearly all leading corporate in India are involved in corporate social responsibility (CSR) programmes in areas like education, health, sports, livelihood creation, skill development, women development and empowerment of weaker sections of the society. Special efforts have come from the Tata Group, Infosys, Bharti Enterprises, Coca Cola India, Pepsico, India Cements and ITC.

Four Indians, including Sunil Mittal, Chairman and Managing Director of the Bharti Group, non -resident Indian Anil Agarwal, Shiv Nadar HCL Technologies Chairman and non government organization activist Rohini Nilekani were featured in the Forbes list of '48 Heroes of Philanthropy'.

Sunil Mittal

Shiv Nadar

Anil Agarwal

Rohini Nilekani

India has been named among the top ten Asian countries paying increasing importance towards corporate social responsibility (CSR) disclosure norms.India was ranked fourth in the list, according to social enterprise CSR Asia's Asian Sustainability Ranking (ASR).

> Social obligation is much bigger than supporting worthy causes.
>
> – William Ford Jr., Chairman, Ford Motor Co

In another study undertaken by automotive research company, TNS Automotive, India has been ranked second in global corporate social responsibility. The study was based on a public goodwill index and India received 119 points in the index against a global average of 100. Thailand was at the top slot with 124 points.

Although corporate India is involved in CSR activities, the central government is working on a framework for quantifying the CSR initiatives of companies to promote them further. One of the ways to attract companies towards CSR work is to develop a system of CSR credits, similar to the system of carbon credits which are given to companies for green initiatives.

The government is also finalizing plans to ensure that public sector companies also participate actively in CSR initiatives. The Department of Public Enterprises has come out with guidelines for central public sector enterprises to take up important corporate social responsibility projects to be funded by 2-5 per cent of the company's net profits.

> Out of all those millions and millions of planets floating around there in space, this is our planet, this is our little one, so we just got to be aware of it and take care of it.
>
> – Paul McCartney

CSR activities carried out by Companies in India

Reliance Industries and Tata Group firms –

Tata Motors and Tata Steel – are known for their corporate social responsibility initiatives in the field of education, environment conservation and public health, according to a survey.

IBM joined hands with the Tribal Development Department of Gujarat for a development project aimed at upliftment of tribals in the Sasan area of Gir forest.

Many IT and ITES took various initiatives including application of renewable energy technologies, moving to paperless operations and recognition of environmental standards.

HSBC India, Max New York Life and Standard Chartered Bank and Telecom operators including Airtel, Aircel, Vodafone and Idea, took a decision of asking their customers to shift to e-statements and e-receipts and save paper.

State-owned navratna company Coal India Ltd (CIL) invested US$67.5 million in 2010-11 on social and environmental causes. Public sector aluminium company NALCO has contributed US$3.23 million for development work in Orissa's Koraput district as part of its CSR.

> You cannot depend on your eyes when your imagination is out of focus.
>
> – Mark Twain

Mangalore Refinery and Petrochemicals Limited (MRPL) spent Rs 12.70 crore on various CSR activities during 2009-10. NASSCOM Foundation, the social development arm of NASSCOM, in partnership with Microsoft announced Connect IT Workshops for NGOs and government officials in Karnataka.

As part of its CSR, pharmaceutical major GlaxoSmithKline (GSK) dedicated its new Albendazole manufacturing unit in its existing Nashik facility to the World Health Organization's (WHO) global programme to eliminate lymphatic filariasis (LF).

National Thermal Power Corporation (NTPC) announced that it will set up a medical college and an engineering college in Orissa as part of its CSR activities.

In recognition of its commitment to energy conservation and efficiency, Jindal Steel and Power Limited's (JSPL) Raigarh (Chhattisgarh)-based plant has been conferred with the National Energy Conservation Award (NECA) 2010.

> There are two ways to live your life. One is as though nothing is a miracle. The other is as though everything is a miracle.
>
> Albert Einstein

PVR Nest, the CSR arm of PVR Ltd, was 'highly commended' under the Best Green Educational Project category (promoting sustainable development issues) at the Global Green Award 2010 in London.

New Delhi Municipal Council (NMDC) was felicitated and conferred with Pragya Puraskar for its outstanding initiatives towards CSR activities for socio-economic and cultural upliftment of weaker sections in the society.

Tata Power, Mahindra and Mahindra, IBM India and Hindalco Industries became recipients of the Golden Peacock Global Awards for corporate social responsibility, at Lisbon in Portugal.

List of projects for funding under CSR:

- Any other programme addressing local needs of the area community in pursuance of the overall objectives
- Backward and forward linkages for improving livelihood of the economically weaker sections.
- Climate change preparedness, preventive measures and capacity building for disaster management.
- Conservation and taping of new and renewable sources of energy such as wind power, solar energy, biomass based energy, etc.
- Conservation of natural resources, e.g., rain water hartvesting, reducing carbon foot print, etc.
- Improvement in sanitation, public health and hygiene
- Model projects and consultancies for assessing new ventures.

> The major problems in the world are the result of the differences between the way nature works and the way people think.
>
> – Gregory Bateson

- Organisation health and family welfare camps.
- Pillot projects in areas where special intervention is required.
- Promotion of education, training and skill development (particularly community based).
- Skill/ efficiency improvement of members of cooperatives.
- Visits to successful cooperatives.

> We abuse land because we regard it as a commodity belonging to us. When we see land as a community to which we belong, we may begin to use it with love and respect.
>
> – Aldo Leopold

How to implement CSR commitments

Every firm has its own way of implementing CSR and here are some commonly accepted ways of implementing CSR.

1. Develop an integrated CSR decision-making structure

It is true that every firm is different, each has its own decision-making structure to ensure that it meets its commitments and customer needs. Yet it is essential that the firm align its CSR goals and decision making with its overall goals and strategies, so that taking CSR considerations into account in corporate decision making becomes as natural as taking customer perspectives into account.

2. Prepare and implement a CSR business plan

Develop and implement the CSR business plan, which should flow from the CSR strategy and commitments. The CSR business plan should be separately described as part of the company's existing overall business plan. CSR business plan helps to ensure that the words are transformed into action.

> I believe it to be perfectly possible for an individual to adopt the way of life of the future. . . without having to wait for others to do so.
> Mahatma Gandhi

3. Set targets and measure the performance

At times it is not possible to measure the targets. In such cases a qualitative target is used to measure. CSR activities can be measured by getting feedback from various stakeholders.

4. Engage people within the organisation

Implementation of CSR depends on the employees of the organisation. These are the people who act as ambassadors and are the people who come up with lot of new ideas and strategies. They should be educated or else they prove to be a problem. Ensure good communication between employees, their representatives and the management

5. Provide CSR training

Companies need to train employees involved in CSR activities. Proper training ensures that employees have information on the firm's CSR commitments, programs and implementation. This is very much useful when training employees belonging to various regions.

Books for further reading

- Global Practices of Corporate Social Responsibility, Samuel O. Idowu and Walter Leal Filho , Springer; Soft cover reprint of hardcover 1st ed. 2009 edition (November 10, 2010).
- A Future for Everyone: Innovative Social Responsibility and Community Partnerships, David Maurrasse, Routledge, 19-Feb-2004
- Corporate Social Responsibility and International Development: Is Business the Solution?, Michael Hopkins, Earthscan, 2007.
- What Matters Most: How A Small Group of Pioneers Is Teaching Social Responsibility To Big Business, and Why Big Business Is Listening, Jeffrey Hollender, Stephen Fenichell, Basic Books, 03-Jan-2006.
- The Responsibility Revolution: How the Next Generation of Businesses Will Win, Jeffrey Hollender et al, John Wiley & Sons, 15-Mar-2010.
- Professionals' Perspectives of Corporate Social Responsibility, Samuel O. Idowu, Walter Leal Filho, Springer, 01-Oct-2009.
- Perspectives on Corporate Social Responsibility, Nina Boeger, Edward Elgar Publishing, 01-Nov-2008.
- Corporate Social Responsibility: Doing the Most Good for Your Company and Your Cause, Philip Kotler, Nancy Lee, John Wiley & Sons, 29-Sep-2008.
- Corporate Social Responsibility: The Good, the Bad and the Ugly, Subhabrata Bobby Banerjee, Edward Elgar Publishing, 2007.
- Corporate Social Responsibility: A Case Study Approach, Chris A. Mallin, Edward Elgar Publishing, 01-Jan-2009.
- Environmental Protection and the Social Responsibility of Firms: Perspectives from Law, Economics, and Business, Bruce L. Hay et al., Resources for the Future, 06-Apr-2005.
- Managing Corporate Social Responsibility in Action: Talking, Doing and Measuring, Frank Den Hond et al., Ashgate Publishing, Ltd., 2007.
- Learning, Work and Social Responsibility: Challenges for Lifelong Learning in a Global Age, Karen Evans, Springer, 01-Jun-2009.

17 Professional Ethics

LEARNING OUTCOME

- Introduction
- Meaning & Definition
- Profession
- What is Professional?
- Professionalism:
- Professional Ethics
- Implementation of Ethical Code
- Core value of acting with professional Ethics:
- Five basic assumptions underpin the understanding of ethics:
- Need for Professional ethics
- Two aspects of professional ethics
- Model Code of Professional Ethics that could be implemented in an organisation
- Some of the best practices with regard to professional ethics
- Most trusted Profession in India
- Books for further reading

> If you once forfeit the confidence of your fellow citizens, you can never regain their respect and esteem. Abraham Lincoln

Introduction

Professional ethics in an organization would mean a set of values, principles and morals followed in the best defined manner. It is theses codes of ethics that define what is right and what is wrong, which decision to take and which one to leave. How much can you flex and how much to restrict. Taking professional and ethical decisions aren't always easy.

Professional code of ethics can be defined as, set of principles that all employees must comply and ensure ethical decision making even in difficult situations.

Professional code of ethics is said to be the base platform for every employee to build his career on. Employees define different criteria's, and exceptions based on the heterogeneous situations.

Under the definition of professional code of conduct, an unethical behavior can cost a lot to the company. It will not only bring bad name to the project, organization but can also sabotage the employee's career. If the employees of the organization do not behave professionally on ethics it will reflect badly on the organizations image which can be very damaging overall.

> The first step in the evolution of ethics is a sense of solidarity with other human beings.
> Albert Schweitzer

It is always advised that the organization must set very high standards for professional code of ethics in order to maintain a stance of trust as well as integrity for which everyone is liable to and everyone can benefit from. This code of professional ethics once imbibed in the culture, always reflects various aspects of their live.

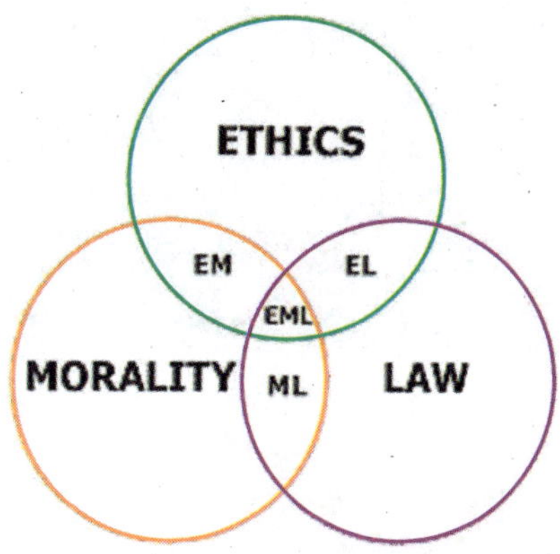

The concept of Professional Ethics is partly comprised of what a professional should or should not do in the work place. It also encompasses a much greater part of the professionals life. If a professional is to have ethics then that person needs to adopt that conduct in all of his dealings. Computer Societies around the world such as the IEEE and national bodies in Australia, Singapore, the UK and other countries have on their websites professional codes of ethics to consider and adopt in the way professionals conduct themselves in and out of the work place. Things that are included are concepts like: professional respect, avoidance of dishonest or fraudulent activity such as plagiarism and the professional development of the individual. Another aspect of this is the enhancement of the profession and the industry within which the professional works. This concerns a professional's conduct and behaviour while carrying out their professional work. This then, is work for the good of the community and mankind.

> The only ones among you who will be really happy are those who will have sought and found how to serve. Albert Schweitzer

Meaning

Profession

- Group identity
- Shared education, training -- requirements for admission
- Special uncommon knowledge
- Knowledge used in the service of others... positive social need
- Involves individual judgment, (some) autonomy in decisions
- Adherence to certain values
- Penalties for substandard performance
- Matter of degree ... there are many "emerging professions".
- Obstacle in the way of the OHS professional is the diverse nature of practice with competing co-professionals.
- You are not a professional until you are a member of a group of colleagues who have articulated a set of standards and values and can enforce them, at the very least, by exclusion from the group.

> Honesty is the cornerstone of character. Honesty pays dividends both in dollars and in peace of mind. B.C. Forbes

What is Professional?

- Possesses specialized knowledge and skills
- Belongs to and abides by the standards of a society
- Serves an important aspect of the public good

Professionalism:

- Skill, competency in work
- Relational element – work will be beneficial to others
- Work itself doesn't have moral status
- Execution of work has moral status
- Recognizing when We're in the Realm of Ethics

Watch the language:

- Right and wrong -- Actions
  Good and bad -- Motives, methods, goals

What shall you profit, if you shall gain the whole world, and lose your own soul? Bible, Mark 8:36

Professional Ethics

- the study of what we do in our professional lives
- Purpose... Helps professional decide when faced with a problem that raises a moral issue
- Complexity ... Can be many people, with many issues involved ... may be involved history to the issues ... may be an issue WHO decides, not just WHAT decided.
- moral expectations specific to the occupational group, tend to focus on concrete "bottom up" cases
- Professional ethics the ethical norms, values, and principles that guide a profession and the ethics of decisions made within the profession.
- professional ethics liability,

1. The obligation of all professionals to their clients to do no harm.
2. The legal obligation of health care professionals, or their insurers, to compensate patients for injury or suffering caused by acts of omission or commission by the professionals.

- Professional Ethics is partly comprised of what a professional should or should not do in the work -place. It also encompasses a much greater part of the professional's life. If a professional is to have ethics then that person needs to adopt that conduct in all of his dealings. Another aspect of this is the enhancement of the profession and the industry within which the professional works.

Pain is inevitable; suffering is optional. Buddhist proverb

- All persons, whether in business, government, educational institutes, or any other professions are concerned with ethics. Encyclopedia of Social Sciences defines ethics as "the organization or criticism of conduct in terms of notions like, good, right or welfare... Ethics is the secular and critical manner of taking account of the rationalizing process in human conduct. Its temper is non-mystical, and its orientation is social rather than theological."

Implementation of Ethical Code

Theodore Parcel and James Weber suggest that this can be accomplished in three ways:

- By establishing appropriate company policy or a code of Ethics.
- By using a formally appointed ethics

committee.

- By teaching ethics in management development programmes.

The most common way to institutionalize ethics is to establish a code of ethics; much less common is the use of ethics board committees.

> To know what is right and not do it is the worst cowardice. Confucius

Code of Ethics	Code of conduct
general	specific
values/principles judgement	prescriptions/ directives
"empowering"	uniformity
"aspirational"	enforceable statement of something specific

Core value of acting with professional Ethics:

1. Act with integrity. Never put your own gain above the welfare of your clients or others to whom you have a professional responsibility. Respect their confidentiality at all times and always consider the wider interests of society in your judgements.

2. Always be honest. Be trustworthy in all that you do – never deliberately mislead, whether by withholding or distorting information.

3. Be open and transparent. Share the full facts with your clients, making things as plain and intelligible as possible.

4. Be accountable. Take full responsibility for your actions, and don't blame others if things go wrong.

5. Act within your limitations. Be aware of the limits of your competence and don't be tempted to work beyond these. Never commit to more than you can deliver.

6. Be objective at all times. Give clear and appropriate advice. Never let sentiment or your own interests cloud your judgement.

7. Always treat others with respect. Never discriminate against others.

8. Set a good example. Remember both your public and private behaviour could affect your own, and other members' reputations.

9. Have the courage to make a stand. Be prepared to act if you suspect a risk to safety or malpractice of any sort.

> No one has ever become poor by giving. Anne Frank

Five basic assumptions underpin the understanding of ethics:

- **Professional ethics is a process.** Ethics are not a fixed text to be learnt once. It is a way of reviewing
- **Behaviour against constantly changing standards.** What may be ethical today, or in a particular society, may be viewed differently by others or at another time.
- **Human behaviour is caused.** There is a motive for all human behaviour eg,

financial gain, power, compassion.

- Actions have consequences. The equivalent of Newton's Third Law of Physics – 'Every force has an equal and opposite reaction'.
- What is ethical depends on the individual's point of view. This is influenced by a variety of factors including published codes and statements.
- **Good ethical business practice rests on mutual vulnerability.** We are each susceptible to the actions of others, and the way we are treated depends on how we treat others. Respect is not a right and must be earned.

> If you're not part of the solution, you're part of the problem.
> – Eldridge Cleaver

Need for Professional ethics

1. Protecting the stakeholders

The need for professional ethics is based upon the vulnerability of others. All the stakeholders must be protected from exploitation in a situation in which they are unable to protect themselves which may due to the lack the relevant knowledge to do.

Ethics means a code of conduct that directs an individual in dealing with others. Business Ethics is a form of the skill that examines ethical moralities and honesty or ethical problems that can arise in a business environment. It deals with matters regarding morals, principles, duties and corporate governance applicable to a company and its employees, customers, shareholders, media, suppliers, government and dealers.

This is what the famous Henry Kravis had to say about professional ethics: "If you don't have integrity, you have nothing. You can't buy accountability. You can have all the money in the world, but if you are not a moral and ethical person, you really have nothing."

> A lie has speed, but truth has endurance. Edgar J. Mohn

2. Establishing core management practice

Ethics are also related to the core of management practices such as human resource management, accounting information, production, sales and marketing, intellectual property knowledge and skill, international business and economic systems.

In the corporate world, the organization's culture sets standards for shaping the difference between good or bad, right or wrong and fair or unfair. This quote by Albert Einstein says it all: "Relativity applies to physics, not ethics." The point being that it is possible to make profits without having to negotiate on ethics. And over and above the factor of correctness associated with ethics, an ethical business and its proprietors only serve themselves, their clients and the whole enterprise much better in the final reckoning.

3. Advantage of being an ethical person/company

A business is successful to the extent that it provides a product or service that contributes to happiness in all of its form. This quote by Mihaly Csikszentmihalyi is a fitting description of this reality.

Thus, ethics are important not only in business but in all the other parts of life because it is an important base on which a civilized and cultured society is built. A business or society without ethics is only headed towards self-destruction.

Dreams are what get you started. Discipline is what keeps you going.
Jim Ryun

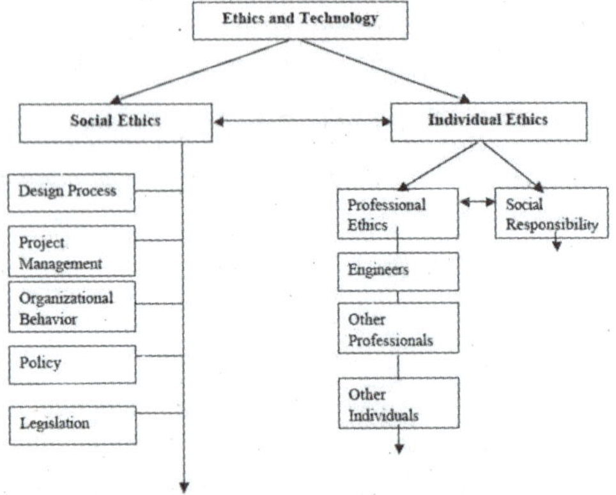

Two aspects of professional ethics

Though the ethical values differ from person to person, there are two generally accepted standards.

1. **Compulsory standard:** The mandatory standards must apply to all grades of employees working for an organization. It must be adhered to for professional, legal and ethical reasons. Penalty to the violation of any of these standards must also be an integral part of the compulsory standard.
2. **Ideal Standard:** The ideal standard would be defined as the best benchmarking standard and employees must strive to reach up to that level.

To ignore evil is to become an accomplice to it.
Martin Luther King, Jr

Model Code of Professional Ethics that could be implemented in an organisation

I. Purpose and Scope

This Code of Professional Ethics lays down the standards of integrity, professionalism and confidentiality which all members of the Association shall be bound to respect in their work as conference interpreters.

II. Code of Honour

Members of the Association shall be bound by the strictest secrecy, which must be observed towards all persons and with regard to all information disclosed in the course of the practice of the profession at any gathering not open to the public.

III. Working Conditions

Members of the association shall be liable to be provided with working condition as per the law.

IV. Amendment Procedure

The Code may be modified by a decision taken with a two-thirds majority of votes cast and, if appropriate, after having sought a legal opinion on the proposals.

Our is a world of nuclear giants and ethical infants.
General Omar Bradley

Some of the best practices with regard to professional ethics

1. Do provide respect to others.

2. Do things for the good of yourself, the customer and the profession.

3. Do ask for help in order to meet the project or task deadline.

4. Do be honest in your work by telling the client, customer, or boss.

5. Do deliver quality in a timely fashion.

6. Do return value to your community locally and globally

7. Do return value to your customer in all business decisions

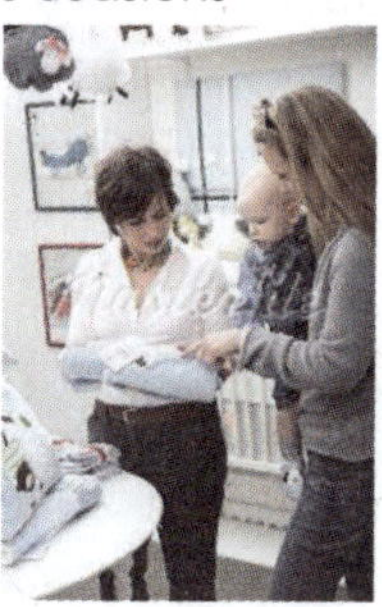

8. Treat others as a professional and they will treat you like one too.

9. Promote your profession.

10. Start using words like we, us and ours.

> "Business social responsibility should not be coerced; it is a voluntary decision that the entrepreneurial leadership of every company must make on its own."
> – John Mackey

Most trusted Profession in India

1. Teacher
2. Fire fighter
3. Farmer
4. Scientist
5. Member of the armed forces
6. Doctor
7. Pilot
8. Surgeon
9. Nurse
10. Engineer
11. Dentist
12. Software engineer
13. Chef
14. Architect
15. Pharamist
16. Paramedic
17. Bus/train driver
18. Veterinarian
19. Banker
20. Economist
21. Hair dresser
22. Flight attendant
23. Electrician
24. CEO
25. Mechanic
26. Accountant
27. Judge
28. Financial planner
29. Plumber
30. Journalist
31. Tour guide
32. Domestic helper
33. Taxi driver
34. Hawker
35. Religious leader
36. Lawyer
37. Police officer
38. Government official
39. Real estate agent
40. Politician.

SOURCE: Reader's Digest March 2010

Top Ten Work Ethics

1.	Attendaance	Be on time... don't be absent!!
2.	Appearance	Clothe well... remain hygiene ... Have manners
3.	Attitude	Be positive ... stay focused
4.	Respect	Be sensitive to unity in diversity
5.	Character	Be honest ... Dependable ... Loyal

6.	Cooperation	Work together to achieve more
7.	Communication	Be good at written ... Verbal ... visual
8.	Team Work	Work towards a common goal
9.	Productivity	Make use of your time... resources ... talents
10.	Organizational skills	Ensure that collectively too you are good

Books for further reading

- Ethics for the Professions, John R. Rowan and Jr. Samuel Zinaich, Wadsworth Publishing; June 13, 2002.
- Ethics Across the Professions: A Reader for Professional Ethics, Clancy Martin et al, Oxford University Press, USA ,October 16, 2009.
- The Ethics of Professional Practice, Richard D. Parsons, Allyn & Bacon; 1 edition, October 5, 2000.
- An Essay on Professional Ethics, George Sharswood, Fili-Quarian Classics, July 12, 2010.
- Professional Ethics: Power and Paradox, Karen Lebacqz, Abingdon Press, January, 1985.
- Professional Ethics, Michael D. Bayles, Wadsworth Pub Co; 2 Sub edition, July 1988.
- Professional Ethics, George Sharswood, Xinware Corporation, October 6, 2007.
- Textbook on Professional Ethics and Human Values, R.S. Naagarazan, New Age International, 01-Jan-2007.
- Professional Ethics and Human Values, A. Alavudeen et al, Firewall Media, 01-Jan-2008.
- Human Values and Professional Ethics, Vaishali R Khosla and Kavita Bhagat, Technical Publications, 01-Jan-2009.
- Human Values & Professional Ethics, Dr. Pushpendra Singh et al, Krishna Prakashan Media, 2002.
- The Ground of Professional Ethics, Daryl Koehn, Routledge, 20-Dec-1994.
- Professional ethics: power and paradox, Karen Lebacqz, Abingdon Press, 1985.
- Professional ethics: the consultant professions and their code, Francis Alan Roscoe Bennion, Knight, 01-Aug-1969.
- Examples & Explanations: Professional Responsibility 3rd Edition, W. Bradley Wendel, Aspen Publishers; 3 edition, November 24, 2010.
- Professional Ethics and Civic Morals, Émile Durkheim, Routledge, 22-Apr-1992.
- Professional Ethics and Social Responsibility, Daniel E. Wueste, Rowman & Littlefield, 01-Oct-1994.

18 Workplace/Office Politics

LEARNING OUTCOME

- Introduction - What is a workplace?
- What is workplace politics?
- Good workplace politics Vs Bad workplace politics.
- Inevitability of workplace politics
- Reasons for workplace Politics
- Workplace politics people play at work
- The effects of workplace politics
- Navigating/Making Workplace politics to your favour
- Handling Workplace politics
- How to avoid the office politics?
- Practising Positive Workplace Politics
- Workplace politics – The Man & The Animal Connection
    - The Fox People
    - The Owl People
    - The Sheep People
    - The Mule People
- Books for further reading

> "The Roots of Violence: Wealth without work, Pleasure without conscience, Knowledge without character, Commerce without morality, Science without humanity, Worship without sacrifice, Politics without principles." will ruin the world.
>
> – Mahatma Gandhi

Introduction - What is a workplace?

A place where persons from various backgrounds, different educational qualifications and varied interests come together to work towards a common goal is called a workplace. In other words a workplace is a place where people are paid to do work.

And people must work as a single unit to avoid unnecessary conflicts and politics at the workplace to ensure efficiency and productivity. In order to attain greatness at the work place, the people should develop a sense of belongingness and dedication towards their work.

A sense of unity is important in order to give the best in the place where you work. It is also imperative for the people to work together in close coordination with the fellow worker. But it is not so in the real scenario.

> "There are but two means of locomotion to the top. Either people must like you so much that they push you there, or you, yourself, are so good that you push yourself there". - Gerald Sparrow
>
> – Mahatma Gandhi

Workplace, in fact, is filled with lot of politics. People stand divided on four grounds – region or religion, and caste or creed. The division is so much that at times it leads people to take extreme steps.

The terms workplace politics and office politics are understood to be the same and hence the first term workplace politics only is used in the coming pages for the convenience of the readers.

What is workplace politics?

In its purest form, workplace politics is simply about getting from here to there: securing a promotion, seeing an idea come to a reality, or gaining support to make an organizational change. But workplace politics is often tagged with a negative connotation.

Workplace politics could be understood as "the use of power by an individual for the purpose of obtaining advantage beyond the accepted limit". Those advantages could be monetary or non-monetary. In other words, it means how the power vested with an individual is put into use. It is the strategy people employ to take advantage of the situation that prevails particularly at the expense of others.

Workplace politics are the strategies that people play to gain advantage, personally or for a cause they support. In short, workplace politics can be said as "the use and misuse of power in the workplace".

Good workplace politics Vs Bad workplace politics.

Good office politics can help you promote yourself and your cause and more often it can be achieved by good networking.

> "The person who says "I'm not political" is in great danger.... Only the fittest will survive, and the fittest will be the ones who understand their office's politics."
>
> – Jean Hollands

Bad workplace politics causes commotion and confusion. It generally adversely affects the working environment and relationships within in.

Inevitability of workplace politics

There is no place in the world where there is no workplace politics. In spite of the fact that people may belong to same region, religion, caste or creed still people stand divided on some or the other ground. In such cases, the reasons for getting into workplace politics could be to

- Get ahead
- Gain information
- Gain power
- Control resources
- Dominate over other people
- Get others to do things you want done

> "Politics is for the present, but an equation is for eternity."
>
> – Albert Einstein

- There are also few other reasons why people indulge in workplace politics. They are listed below.
- Some people have more power than the others through hierarchy or position they hold
- For some people, getting promotion is important, and this causes workplace politics
- Some people opt for popular decisions rather than right decision that is decisions are often not work-related
- People have to compete for limited resources

The above mentioned points go on to prove that however big or small the organisations are, there is bound to be workplace politics.

Reasons for Workplace Politics

You don't need to have worked in an office for years together to know what workplace politics is. Anyone who has had a short stint at any job would know what workplace politics is. There is no place in the world where there is no workplace politics. Workplace politics has become a problem to reckon with. According to a survey 18% of an administrator's time is consumed in tackling/resolving workplace politics. Here are some major reasons why people indulge in workplace politics.

- people aspiring to come to limelight without much hard work
- people aspiring to achieve something beyond their given power
- absence or lack of supervision and control at the workplace.
- too much of gossip at work lead to politics.
- arrogant superiors
- inferior or unqualified staff
- Jealous colleagues

> "Politics is the art of preventing people from sticking their noses in things that are properly their business."
> – Paul Valery

Workplace politics people play at work

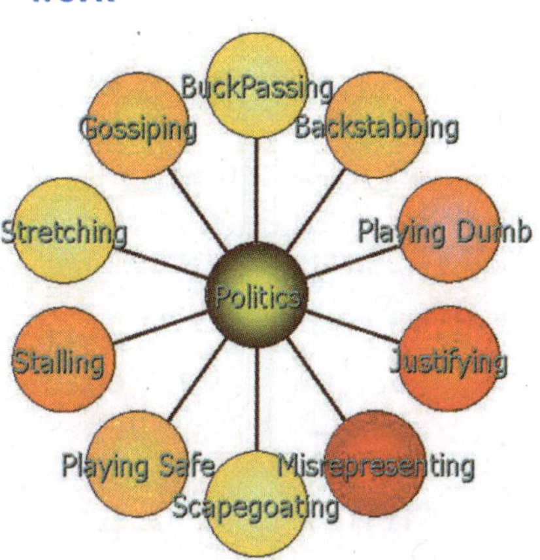

As mentioned earlier, people are divided on the grounds of region, religion, caste or creed. And so the kind of workplace politics people indulge in and the political games that people play vary from region to region, religion to religion, caste to caste and creed to creed. However the game people play can be classified into legitimate and illegitimate.

Legitimate

- Rational persuasion
- Consultation
- Favour exchange
- Personal appeal
- Coalition

Illegitimate

- Backstabbing
- Blackmail
- Buck Passing
- Gossiping
- Justifying
- Misrepresenting
- Playing Dumb
- Playing Safe
- Pressure
- Sabotage
- Scapegoating
- Stalling
- Stretching
- Symbolic protests
- Threats
- Whistle-blowing

> "Politics is supposed to be the second oldest profession. I have come to realize that it bears a very close resemblance to the first."
> – Ronald Reagan

The effects of workplace politics

Besides causing problems to the individuals, the end result of a workplace politics can be far more devastating. Since the employees and managers concentrate on the workplace politics, they have less time to pay attention to their jobs. This causes fall in production, productivity and financial loss which may in turn cause closure of business.

- affects the relationship amongst the individuals
- difficult to concentrate on work
- increases conflicts and tensions at the workplace
- increases the degree of criticism level and people tend to crib more
- office politics promotes negativity at the work place
- people do not enjoy at the workplace and treat work as a burden
- people stop helping and trusting each other
- reduces the productivity of individuals
- the organization is at a loss

Navigating/Making Workplace politics to your favour

Workplace politics is often understood to be something that needs less or no attention. But the truth is, particularly in the present materialistic world, to ensure your own success, you need to learn to navigate it. If someone is going ignore workplace politics that goes around you, he may suffer while the others may take unfair and undue advantage.

So it is clear that if you avoid good workplace politics, you may miss the opportunities to further you and your friends' interest.

> "Politics is war without bloodshed while war is politics with bloodshed."
> – Mao Tse-Tung

To deal with workplace politics and use it to your favour , first accept the reality of it. Then need to develop strategies to deal with the political behaviour that is going on around you. The ideal way is to be a good observer and then use the information you gather to build a strong network to operate in. Here are some important tips to make workplace for your favour. Find out

- Are there groups that have formed?
- How does the influence flow between the parties?
- Who are the real influencers?
- Who gets along with whom?
- Who has the authority?
- Who has the most trouble getting along with others?
- Who is "the brains behind the organization"?
- Who is involved in interpersonal conflict?
- Who is respected?
- Who mentors whom?

> Moral excellence comes about as a result of habit.
> We become just by doing just acts, temperate by doing temperate acts, brave by doing brave acts
> –Aristotle

Handling Workplace politics

Generally you find people who are brilliant just cannot get ahead in their workplace. You also find people who are extraordinarily talented never understand how some of the crucial decisions are taken in their workplace, how the informal teams are formed and how the corporate cultures work.

However a research reveals that many people who get ahead in their workplace are solid performers, highly effective, and capable of handling increased responsibility. What's the secret?

You need not to be an expert to handle workplace politics. You just need to observe, understand and apply your mind. You need to use/leverage your innate talents. You need to learn the technique of dealing with workplace politics because there is no place without it. You have to face the reality of workplace politics or else you may experience a lifelong frustration. Susan Roane in her article says"A keen sense of office politics can have a dramatic effect on our businesses and careers," . Many people fail at work because of their inability to deal with workplace politics and not because they do not have the requisite skills to succeed in their jobs.

> "Politics: the unwritten rules of how things are done or not done."
> Pat McBride, The Black Collegian

Online author Barbara defines workplace politics as "the way in which workers recognize, and seek to reconcile, their competing interests." No matter the size of your company, country, or association, all politics are local. In other words, your workplace politics define who gets noticed and rewarded. Therefore, mastering workplace politics will help you understand how things are done in your office. Here are some ways in which you can handle workplace politics.

1. The choice is yours

You are left with only two options – either you fight or flight. Fight reactions will cause more resistance to whatever you try to achieve. Flight reactions will give the impression that you are a pushover and there is a possibility of being taken for granted by others. Neither option seems to be healthy for career growth.

2. Be aware of what you want to achieve

Since fight or flight do not seem to be good for the organisations, it is better to chose an option that suits best for the business. Ultimately everyone wants the business to be successful. If the business fails then everybody fails. Keep the organisation's interest first.

3. Work on your circle of influence

Instead of feeling angry or sad about the situation focus on the things that can come handy to you. Namely work on your circle of influence. This is said to be the best way to overcome the feelings of helplessness. It enables others to understand the way you operate within the given constraints.

> "Stop pretending that it doesn't exist... Decrying the fact the system is political is like complaining that water is wet"
>
> – Gerard Egan

4. Stay neutral

In workplace politics, you always land up in a dilemma of whom to support. You often find yourself stuck in between two power centres who are at odds with each other. You find yourself like a shuttle cock beaten from both the sides. In cases like this, focus on the common good and don't take side with either of them – even if you like one better than the other. Place them on a common communication platform and ensure open communications among all parties.

5. Do not personalize the issues

There are times where you will feel like giving your opponent your piece of mind and there by teach him a lesson. You should never do that. Never personalize the issues because what goes around comes around, especially at the work place. To win in the office, you have to build a network of people which you can tap into.

Even if you are a star performer, your boss will have to fight a political uphill battle if other managers or peers see you as someone who is difficult to work with. The last thing you'll want is to make it difficult for your boss to champion you for a promotion.

6. Try to understand others before being understood by them

It is human to expect people to first understand you before you understand them. Successful managers and business leaders have learned to suppress this urge.

7. Establish a Win Win approach

Gone are the days where one used to be the winner and the other the loser. In modern business it cannot be the case. It has to be a win win approach. Develop a situation you ensure that you and your competitor win. after all nobody likes to lose.

How to avoid the office politics?

Though it is believed that workplace politics something inevitable, still it can be brought down to a decent level. To ensure that level one follow the points mentioned below.

- Wear No Mask
- Be Transparent
- Flex and Bend
- Listen

- Park the Ego
- Forget the Empire
- Don't Gossip
- Focus On the Business
- Issue at Hand
- Apologize Later

> "Political moves are the navigation through your career – not the driver."
> - Susan DePhillips

Practising Positive Workplace Politics

Be Prepared to Lead

Deal with Rumors Decisively

Ethics and Integrity Do Count

Exploit Smart Tactics

Know How to Deal with the Devious

Know How to Face the Tough Challenges

Manage Your Relationships with the More Powerful

Practice Smart Strategy

Take Responsibility, Not Blame

Understand the Politics of Communication

> Getting along with men isn't what's truly important. The vital knowledge is how to get along with a man, one man.
> – Phyllis McGinley

Workplace politics – The Man & The Animal Connection

Since the origin of man is said to have begun with animals, there is a possibility that man inherited some of the traits from animals. Here is a comparison between the traits associated with the animals and their relevance to human beings.

The Animal Model (courtesy David Bancroft-Turner BA (Hons) MIPD www.tafpi.com)

The Fox People

These are the people who have very political intelligence and they use all their intelligence to achieve their personal goals leaving the organisational goals behind. These are the people who are aware not only the written laws but also the unwritten laws. These are the people who are aware of the formal as well informal ways of doing things and getting things done. These are the people who often play games with hidden agenda.

The Owl People

These are the people who are highly politically intelligent and they use their intelligence to attain both personal as well as organisational goals. They adopt strategies that are good both for them and the organisations. Generally they do not undertake activities that benefit only them.

The Sheep People

These are the people who are said to have a low level of political intelligence and aspirations. These are the ones who are worried about pursuing personal and organisational goals.

These are the people who suspect whole of the political issues that prevail in the organisations. They are of the opinion that workplace politics by all means should be avoided.

The Mule People

These are the people with very low political intelligence and spend all their energies in attaining their personal goals. These are the people who are not aware of the inner politics that take place in the work place. They stuck to their goals and ambitions irrespective of being right or wrong.

> "Politics is perhaps the only profession for which no preparation is thought necessary".
> – Robert Louis Stevenson

In Short

Characteristics associated with Foxes, Owls, Mule and Sheep.

	FOXES
	• Clever • Cunning • Adaptable • Resourceful • Sly • Kill for fun • Furry!

	OWLES
	• Observant • Kill for food • Swift • Silent • Aloof and distant • Wise • Feathery!

	MULES
	• Determined • Hard working • Noisy • Bad tempered • Heavy load carrier • A plodder but sure-footed • Hairy!

	SHEEP
	• Trusting • Innocent • Naïve • Follower • Gentle and timid • Loyal • Woolly!

The facet of the workplace politics cannot be eradicated completely. However, you can learn measures to prevent it so as to lead a peaceful and stress-free office life. A strong work ethic coupled with desire to work with passion can help people to create greater integrity and reduce workplace politics.

Books for further reading

- Quick Skills: Workplace Politics and Personalities, Doris Humphrey, South-Western Educational Pub; I edition, September 25, 2001.
- Secrets to Winning at Office Politics: How to Achieve Your Goals and Increase Your Influence at Work, Marie G. McIntyre, St. Martin's Griffin; 1st edition (June 16, 2005).

- The Secret Handshake: Mastering the Politics of the Business Inner Circle, Kathleen Kelly Reardon Ph.D, Crown Business; Reprint edition (January 15, 2002)
- Workplace Politics, David Bancroft-Turner, Management Pocketbooks (2 Jun 2008)
- Beyond Office Politics: The Hidden Story of Power, Affiliation & Achievement in the Workplace, Linda Sommer, Create Space Independent Publishing Platform (June 14, 2012)
- Office Politics: What They Will Never Tell You, R. Don Steele et al, spb; first edition (June 1, 2011).
- Games At Work: How to Recognize and Reduce Office Politics, Mauricio Goldstein, Jossey-Bass; 1 edition (April 20, 2009)
- Workplace Politics: Survive and Advance, Dr. Donnell Scott, Flyleaf Books, 2010.
- 21 Dirty Tricks at Work: How to Win at Office Politics, Mike Phipps et al, Capstone; 1 edition (September 12, 2005)
- Survival of the Savvy: High-Integrity Political Tactics for Career and Company Success, Rick Brandon, Free Press (November 30, 2004).
- Power, Politics, and Organizational Change: Winning the Turf Game, David Buchanan et al, Sage Publications Ltd; 2nd edition (March 6, 2008)
- Politics in Organizations: Theory and Research Considerations, Gerald R. Ferris et al, Routledge Academic; 1 edition (December 17, 2011).
- Political Skill at Work: Impact on Work Effectiveness, Gerald R. Ferris et al, Nicholas Brealey Publishing; Reprint edition (June 14, 2011)
- Organizational Power Politics: Tactics in Organizational Leadership, Gilbert W. Fairholm, Praeger; 2 edition (August 25, 2009).
- 100+ Tactics for Office Politics (Barron's Business Success), 100+ Tactics for Office Politics (Barron's Business Success),Casey Hawley, Barron's Educational Series; 2 edition (May 16, 2008).

Planning for a Second Career

LEARNING OUTCOME

- Things to be considered for choosing a second career
- Making Your List
- Elements to find in the second career
- Books for further reading

There are some people who never pursue a second career after retiring from a profession in which they may have worked for some substantial years. Many a reasons are attributed for choosing a second career, reasons like utilising your talents, experience, and knowledge are to name some.

A meaningful second career does not happen by a chance. It requires planning for a second career so that it matches your interests, abilities and passion.

Planning for a second career implies embarking on a course of action which will lead to the pursuit of a different job, profession or occupation for a significant number of years having been employed elsewhere.

You can think of second career if you

- are retired from a job on reaching a prescribed age
- are blessed with plenty of spare time in your present job
- are laid off
- working an interim job
- are choosing to retrain for a career that is in demand

Things to be considered for choosing a second career

Kapil Dev as a cricketer – The First Career

Kapil Dev as a Business Man – The Second Career

1. Be qualified

Some careers will require certain qualifications and know-how. If you're really looking for a second career, you will have to go in for such qualifications. Develop the habit of reading widely and be informed of the second career you are seeking for.

2. Know your strengths and weaknesses

You know yourself better than anybody else and should know your strengths and weakness. Knowing your strengths and weaknesses also has to do with your likes and dislikes. If you're someone who doesn't like being bossed around, you'll be better off managing a private business as a second career rather than working for someone.

3. Know how much time you have

Managing two careers may be stressing, hence the need to do all the research needed to choose a second career that won't combine with your first career to overburden you.

You need to rest, sleep and have time for recreational activities like enjoying yourself at the beach, exercising and hanging out with loved ones. Choose a second career that won't overburden or stress you.

4. Consider both mind and heart

Of course, any second career you choose must be one that'll require the use of your brains and in a sense, be creatively fulfilling. You get the chance to use your brain and inherent abilities and know-how.

With regard to your heart, any second career you settle on must also be pleasing to your heart—it must be emotionally fulfilling. If you choose a career you have no love for, you'll definitely and inevitably fall out of love in the near future.

5. Research where jobs are.

It helps to look in fields where there's strong job growth. Fields like healthcare, education and technical consulting services are growing rapidly, with new niches and specialties popping up.

6. Connect with a network.

It helps to find a group of like-minded people who have already gone through such change. You can learn from their firsthand experiences of how they made the move. Talk with people who work in the related fields.

7. Choose a career requiring diverse activities

Any job or career which involves doing one thing in one particular way all the time may become boring and monotonously mundane overtime, hence the need to choose a career requiring different activities. You'll be more excited and motivated in such a career.

8. Evaluate your finances

Your new salary may be far less than you were earning in your first career. As a result, you may need to adjust your lifestyle. As the income is going to decrease you should adjust your standard of living. It would be wise to prepare a financial plan – i.e. the second career financial planning.

9. Age not a barrier

It is never too late to start a second career. There are many examples of late-ages people who made it. KFC owner said to have started it in his late fifties. The issue is not age but personal health, energy level, and having an entrepreneurial spirit. You have to be prepared to meet the challenge of selling yourself, all over again, whether you're starting anew as an employee or starting your own business.

10. Zero in on that perfect second career

Hopefully, you have by now made up your mind on a second career. Go in for it and start earning that second income.

Making Your List

Vijay Amrithraj as Tennis player and Hollywood Film Producer

Planning your second career is a very different exercise from your first career choice. This time, you have the benefit of your work experience and life experience to help you on your way. You are looking for a field that will not only provide an income, but will exercise muscles you may not have flexed ever.

Elements to find in the second career

(a) Are you good at it?

(b) Do you really enjoy that work?

(c) Administrative burden

(d) Travel

(e) Writing

(f) Analytical work

(g) Creativity

(h) Flexibility

To conclude, it's important to note that things may not turn out as you expect in your second career, but there's the need to have patience; things may get better. If the career you choose isn't going well, move on to find a more suitable one and if it is going well, enjoy yourself.

Books for further reading

- Time for a change: how to change your career: the re-entry & re-career workbook, Kent B. Banning, Ardelle F. Friday, VGM Career Horizons, 1995.
- The Mid-Career Success Guide: Planning for the Second Half of Your Working Life, Sally J. Power, Greenwood Publishing Group, 30-Oct-2006.
- Strategic job jumping: fifty very smart tactics for building your career, Julia Hartman, Prima Pub., 01-Jul-1997.
- Back in Control: How to Stay Sane, Productive, and Inspired in Your Career Transition, Diane Grimard Wilson, Sentient Publications, 01-Jun-2004.
- What's Next?: Follow Your Passion and Find Your Dream Job, Kerry Hannon, Chronicle Books, 28-Apr-2010.
- Coach Yourself to a New Career: 7 Steps to Reinventing Your Professional Life, Talane Miedaner, McGraw-Hill Professional, 22-Mar-2010.
- Planning your career change, Kent B. Banning, Ardelle F. Friday McGraw-Hill, 1987
- 10 Career Essentials: Excel at Your Career by Using Your Personality Type, Donna Dunning, Nicholas Brealey Publishing, 16-May-2010 -,
- Career Comeback: Repackage Yourself to Get the Job You Want, Lisa Johnson Mandell, Grand Central Publishing, 07-Jan-2010.
- Ten Laws of Career Reinvention, Pamela Mitchell, Dutton, 31-Dec-2009.
- Career Change: Everything You Need to Know to Meet New Challenges and Take Control of Your Career, David P. Helfand, McGraw-Hill Professional, 11-May-1999.
- Strategies for Successful Career Change: Finding Your Very Best Next Work Life, Martha E. Mangelsdorf, Ten Speed Press, 23-Jun-2009.